Using Technical Analysis

A Step-by-Step Guide to Understanding and Applying Stock Market Charting Techniques

Revised Edition

Clifford Pistolese

McGraw-Hill
New York   San Francisco   Washington, D.C.   Auckland   Bogotá
Caracas   Lisbon   London   Madrid   Mexico City   Milan
Montreal   New Delhi   San Juan   Singapore
Sydney   Tokyo   Toronto

This publication is designed to provide accurate and authoritative information in regard to the subject matter covered. It is sold with the understanding that the author and the publisher are not engaged in rendering legal, accounting, or other professional service.

ISBN 1-55738-527-0

Printed in the United States of America

11 12 13 14 BRBBRB 98 1 0 9 8

McGraw-Hill

A Division of The McGraw·Hill Companies

I dedicate this book to my father, Anthony F. Pistolese. Bull and bear markets can elicit strong emotions in many investors, but your decision making has always been cool-headed and rational. These attributes have contributed to your lifetime of successful investing. You inspired me to develop an analytical approach to the stock market and I will always be grateful for your guidance.

#1 evaluate Price & Volume (Geometry)

2 Volume

3 check Moving Average

4 check IBD for Acumulation/Distribution
Want Low float (Higher Price
A = Accumulation = Good $↑ Rating
E = Distribution = bad $↓

if indicators disagree See Guidelines pg (183)

TABLE OF CONTENTS

LIST OF FIGURES

PREFACE

This book is a guide for the analysis of stock market charts. It explains how to interpret stock price patterns and trends, trading volume, moving averages, accumulation, and distribution information. You'll learn how to analyze these elements to determine what is happening to the price of a stock, and what might happen next.

It's not possible for you to know everything that affects the financial fortunes of a company. However, all that is known about a company's prospects is reflected in the transactions of all the interested parties who buy or sell the company's stock. A summary of the trading activities of these buyers and sellers is published in the newspapers every day. A chart which presents a history of these trading actions reflects all information about the company. By learning to analyze such charts, you'll have access to an excellent source of information for making your buy, hold, and sell decisions.

Chapter 1 outlines the importance of developing the ability to analyze stock charts. The analysis of stock price patterns and trends is explained in Chapters 2 through 8. Chapter 9 presents the concept of moving averages and explains their relationship to trendlines. Chapter 10 introduces the concepts of accumulation and distribution and indicates how these relate to stock price trends and patterns. Performing the simulation exercises in these chapters will help you improve your understanding of the concepts presented.

Chapter 11 provides a series of charts for you to interpret. These charts show price patterns, volume of trading, and moving averages. They also give information on accumulation and distribution. Using all the concepts learned in the preceding chapters, you can test your ability to interpret the meaning of each chart. The correct interpretations are presented so you can check the accuracy of your analyses.

Chapter One

THE CHALLENGE OF THE STOCK MARKET

The stock market can be very confusing. There are thousands of stocks to choose from. Hundreds of advisory letters present conflicting opinions. Many brokers offer their services and advice. There are also experts, analysts, and others in the media who have different points of view. What should an investor do?

COMMON APPROACHES TO STOCK MARKET STRATEGY

Perhaps you have experimented with different methods of beating the market. In these efforts you may have tried one or more of the following common approaches:

- Searching for companies destined for greatness
- Buying popular stocks
- Buying on hot tips
- Fishing for the bottom
- Buying stocks and putting them away

Unfortunately, each of these approaches has serious limitations.

Searching for Companies Destined for Greatness

You've probably heard about stocks which were available for a few dollars a share years ago and are now worth hundreds of times their original prices. While such stories can be inspiring, your chance of achieving that type of success is minuscule. In any young industry, there are many competing companies, but there can be only a couple which will emerge as industry leaders. The rest will join the ranks of the mediocre or go out of business.

The statistics are stacked against you if you hope to find an infant company which will achieve greatness someday. Department of Commerce

1

figures show that more than three out of four new businesses fail within the first three years. They also indicate that the average number of small business failures per year is more than 85,000.

Buying Popular Stocks

Do you make the effort to do your own research, or are you attracted to stocks which receive much attention in the mass media and become popular? If everybody else is buying a stock, it's tempting to jump on the bandwagon.

A popular stock is usually overpriced, because many funds and individuals want to own it. But when today's darling of the investment community falls out of favor, its price declines as the demand dries up along with the evaporation of favorable publicity. The favorites of the investment community change frequently, so buying a popular stock often results in a loss.

Buying on Hot Tips

Passing along hot tips makes for interesting conversations among some investors. As a bull market approaches its top, you may hear many tips. Acting on them, though, is unlikely to provide the reward you anticipate. Here's why:

- There's usually no way to check the validity of the tip. The information may be inaccurate, exaggerated, or, worst of all, completely untrue.

- Even if the story is accurate, you don't know how many people have heard it before you. If you are closer to the end of the line of transmission than to the beginning, you could be buying the stock close to its top.

- The person giving you the tip may have something to gain. If that person owns the stock, he or she is a biased source of information and may be hoping to push up the price by inducing others to buy.

For these reasons hot tips are not a reliable method for making profits.

Fishing for the Bottom

Fishing for the bottom is a phrase used to describe an attempt by an investor to guess where a stock price will stop falling and start rising. He or she places an order to buy at that point. This approach is appealing because it could be a way to buy at a low price. However, once a stock makes a major top and starts dropping, the price usually goes down much further than seems reasonable. Panicked sellers, desperate to cash out, sell their shares "at the market" and force the price lower and lower. In this type of situation, you can't predict how low the price will go. A stock that once sold above $100 per share looks like a bargain at $50. But when the price continues declining to $40, $30, $20, or even lower, $50 is no longer the bargain it appeared to be.

The problem with bottom fishing is there is almost always a valid reason when a stock price goes into a deep decline. Purchasing a stock that has dropped a long way only makes sense if you learn something which may indicate that a recovery in the company's prospects lies directly ahead. Chapter 5, Reversal Formations at Bottoms, can help you detect this type of situation.

Buying Stocks and Putting Them Away

Another approach is to buy a blue chip or other well-recommended stock with the intention of holding it indefinitely. This tactic is based on two assumptions:

- A company which has high profits today will maintain them indefinitely.
- The total return from this investment will outpace any rate of inflation in the long run.

Hoping to select a company which will maintain a high level of profitability for the long run is a guessing game which becomes increasingly difficult as the length of time is extended. An industry with high profit margins today attracts many competitors until those margins shrink drastically. Almost every industry progresses through a life-cycle of highly profitable initial expansion, slowing growth, maturity, and eventual decline. For these reasons, planning to hold a stock forever is more likely to result in a roller coaster ride than in a successful investment.

A More Rewarding Approach to the Stock Market

The approaches described above fail because they are based on unreliable and erroneous information or on fallacious assumptions. If you have tried researching companies, you know how difficult it is to obtain current information about a company and its prospects for the future. (Research reports are available, but have little or no value, because the information they contain is usually already reflected in the price of the stock.) The facts which would be most helpful to know are not available because of SEC regulations about inside information. How, then, do you obtain insight into the current status of and future prospects for a company?

Fortunately, there's a method of investing which is based on all that is known about a company. With this method you can see the impact of that knowledge on the price of the company's stock. This method is called technical analysis.

Through the use of technical analysis you will be able to:

- Interpret stock charts to make more informed decisions on when to buy and when to take your profits

- Determine whether excess demand is likely to push prices up or excess supply is likely to push them down
- Use moving averages to increase your ability to hold stocks for long-term appreciation
- Spot stocks which are being accumulated by better informed investors for long-term capital gains
- Identify stocks which are being distributed (sold) by insiders and other knowledgeable investors

In summary, this approach enables you to analyze what is happening to the price of a stock now and to make a more reliable projection of what may happen to it in the future.

Chapter Two

UPTRENDS

Being able to detect a stock that is starting to rise is the first step toward making a profitable transaction. A stock is rising if it is in an uptrend.

The price of any stock fluctuates in small movements making short-term tops and bottoms over a period of time. When the stock price is charted and the successive bottoms are higher than preceding bottoms, the price is said to be in an *uptrend* (see Figure 2.1). Note that bottom B is higher than bottom A, and bottom C is higher than bottom B. After bottom B was made, the uptrend was established. When bottom C occurred, the uptrend was confirmed. Once bottoms A and B have been made on the chart, you can draw a tentative uptrend line. As each subsequent bottom occurs at or near this line, the uptrend is reconfirmed. The locations of the intervening tops have no significance with respect to the establishment or confirmation of the uptrend.

Once established, the uptrend indicates that for the time being, the forces of demand are stronger than the forces of supply. (The buyers are more anxious than the sellers.) However, this imbalance can change or reverse at any time and when that happens the next bottom may break through the uptrend line. (Refer to point D in Figure 2.1.)

UPTREND BREAKTHROUGH

To be a valid breakthrough, the penetration of the uptrend line should extend below the line by 5 percent of the price of the stock at that point. Thus, if the breakthrough occurs at the price of $50 a share and the price goes to $47.50, this 5 percent decline is enough to represent a breakthrough. However, if the price goes back up the same day and closes at or above $50 per share, the validity of the breakthrough is questionable. In such a situation, you should wait to see whether another penetration meets the 5 percent rule at the close of business for the day. When such a penetration does occur, it is time to sell.

Figures 2.1–2.4
SOME SAMPLES OF UPTRENDS

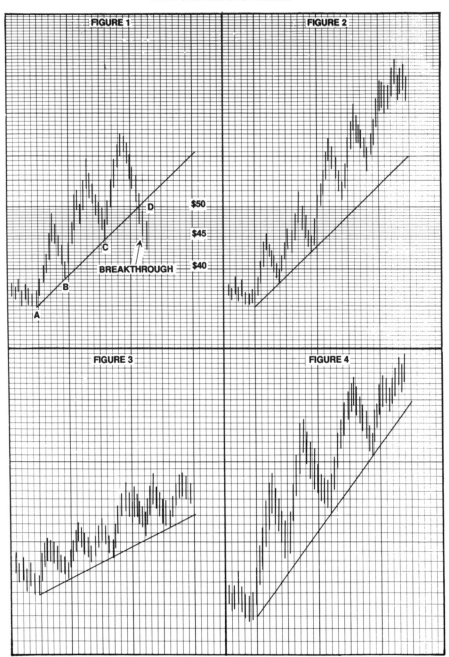

UPTREND VARIATIONS

Uptrends are not always as neat as the one shown in Figure 2.1. Figure 2.2, for example, shows an uptrend pattern that moves from the uptrend line because of sporadic increases in demand for the stock. Uptrends can be very slow (see Figure 2.3), they can be fast (see Figure 2.4), or they can be moderate (as in Figure 2.1). Slow uptrends tend to continue longer than fast ones, and steep uptrends provide opportunities for quick profits.

EXERCISES

In this next section you will participate in some exercises that provide an opportunity to practice identifying uptrends. Review the four figures that follow and decide whether the price action of each stock shows an uptrend. If it does, check the *yes* response in the figure. If it does not, check the *no* response. After indicating your answers, turn to Appendix A, and check your responses.

GUIDELINES FOR USING UPTRENDS

1. Spotting uptrends in the early stages provides excellent opportunities to make profits in the stock market.

2. Once you have bought a stock in an uptrend, it can be held until a definite reversal has occurred.

3. The life span of an uptrend is unpredictable. It can be broken right after it becomes established, or it can continue for months.

Figures 2E.1–2E.4

WHICH ARE UPTRENDS?

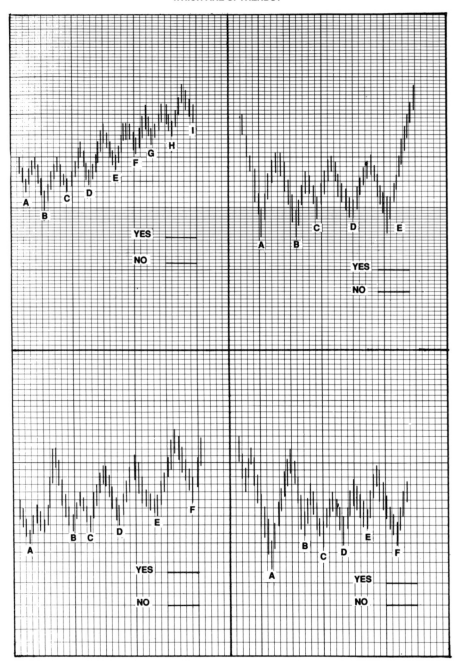

Chapter Three

REVERSAL FORMATIONS AT TOPS

Every company eventually reaches a point at which forces beyond its control stop it from making further progress. As this situation becomes evident to investors, they begin to change their attitude toward the stock of the company. This changing attitude is reflected in the price of the stock as it forms a variety of topping out patterns. This chapter describes those patterns, which are called *reversal formations*.

Before we discuss reversal formations, consider the situation in which an uptrend is followed by a downtrend immediately, without the occurrence of an intervening reversal formation (see Figures 3.1–3.4). These figures show a few of the ways an uptrend can be converted directly into a downtrend. They reflect a sudden change in attitude (from very positive to negative) which is completed in a few days.

The explanation of this sudden change from uptrend to downtrend is as follows. The price has been climbing in conjunction with favorable news or rumors about the company's prospects. Buyers have been anxious to climb aboard a winner, and they continue to pay higher and higher prices because they expect the price to go even higher. At the top (and usually without warning), some bad news about the company's prospects is published or rumored. Then the situation is reversed as the holders of the stock become more anxious to sell than the buyers are to buy. With the supply of the stock for sale suddenly outweighing the demand, the price begins to descend.

Most of the time, however, investors' changes of attitude are more gradual and are reflected in reversal formations that take from two or three months to a year or more to develop and complete. Several types of formations can develop at the end of an uptrend, and we describe those in the following sections.

Figures 3.1–3.4
UPTRENDS CHANGING INTO DOWNTRENDS

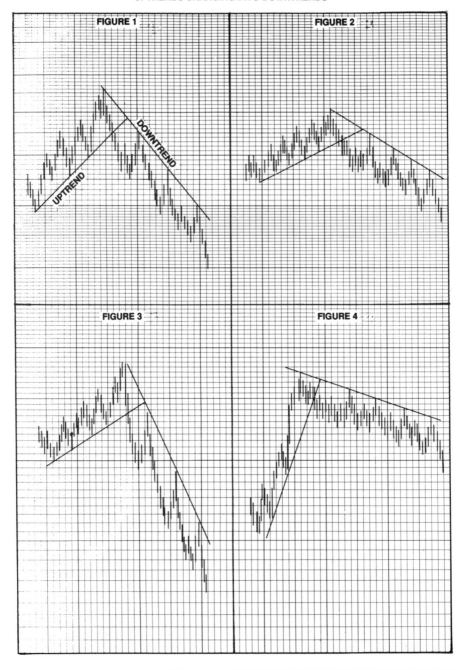

Breakthrough
Long term
HEAD-AND-SHOULDERS FORMATIONS   *Decline*

Head-and-shoulders formations come in a variety of shapes and sizes (see Figures 3.5–3.9). These formations can be tall or short, horizontal or slanted, and have a shoulder on each side. Refer to Figure 3.5, a hypothetical example, as you read the following description of the characteristic features of head-and-shoulders formations.

A head-and-shoulders formation occurs at the end of a long rise in the price of a stock. The formation of the head is usually accompanied by an increase in trading volume. The decline from the top of the head must proceed to a level below the top of the left shoulder before it turns up to form the right shoulder. The neckline can then be drawn across the bottom points of the two valleys between the three peaks. A sell signal is given when the neckline is penetrated to the downside by a distance of 5 percent of the price at that point.

The explanation of a head-and-shoulders formation in terms of buyers' and sellers' hopes and fears is as follows. As the price of the stock goes up, the level of buyer interest tends to increase. More and more buyers place their orders to buy and thus drive the price up with higher volume than usual. Finally, when most buyers have obtained their shares and only a few buyers are left who are willing to buy at the high current price, they become outnumbered by the sellers (at the top of the head). The supply of stock available at these prices exceeds the buyers' interests and prices are driven down (to form the right side of the head). After the price has declined, more buyers decide to buy and they begin to drive the price up to form the right shoulder. As the price approaches the previous high, current holders of the stock, fearful that the price may not return to its previous high, become anxious to sell their shares and are willing to accept prices lower than the preceding peak. When the price fails to regain its old high, the sellers gradually become more fearful that the price will go lower, and a self-fulfilling prophecy is in operation once the neckline is broken. After this breakthrough of the neckline has occurred, there is a good chance that the price of the stock will go into a long-term decline.

Head-and-Shoulders Identification Exercise

Review Figures 3E.1–3E.4. Decide whether the price action of each stock shows a head and shoulders. If you decide price pattern shows a head and shoulders, check the *yes* response in the figure. If the price pattern does not show a head and shoulders, check the *no* response. After indicating your answers, turn to Appendix A, and check your responses.

Figure 3.5
SAMPLE OF HEAD AND SHOULDERS

Figure 3.6

5% Sell now Rule when Break through occurs

Figure 3.7

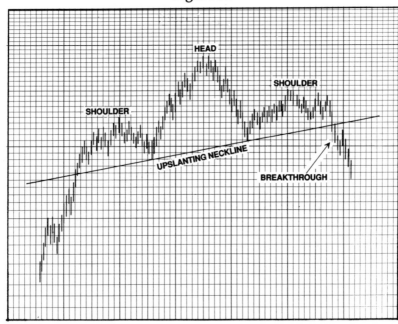

Figure 3.8

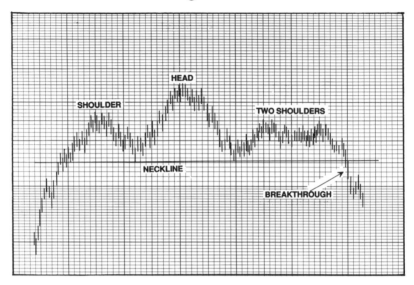

Figure 3.9

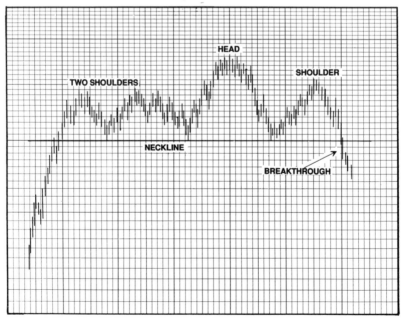

Figure 3E.1

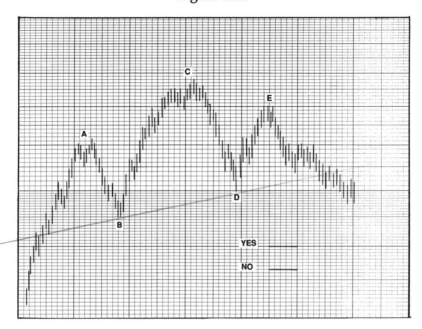

Figure 3E.2

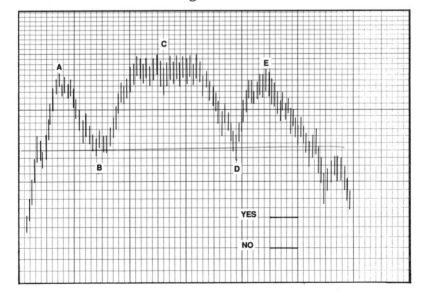

Figure 3E.3

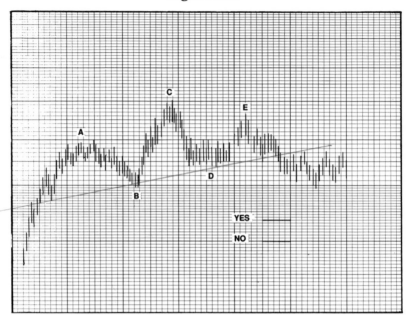

No, must drop below pt A

Figure 3E.4

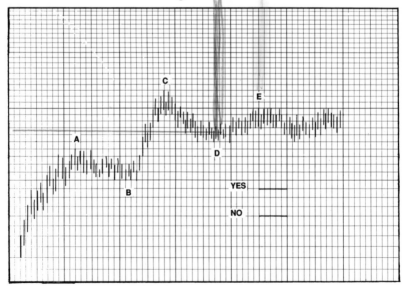

*Break through =
intermed or
Long term decline*

DOUBLE-TOP FORMATIONS

A *double-top formation* occurs when the price of a stock that has peaked once rises again to the same approximate level after a decline, and peaks again. The valley between these peaks may be deep or shallow. The trading volume generated in making the first top will usually be greater than that generated in making the second top. Once the decline from the second top goes 5 percent below the valley floor between the tops, there usually follows a further decline of intermediate or long-term duration (see Figures 3.10–3.14).

In Figures 3.10 and 3.11 the double tops in the price occurred at the same price level. In Figure 3.12 the price at the second top was higher than at the first. In Figures 3.13 and 3.14 the price at the second top was lower than at the first; these slight variations in the height of the two tops are of no particular significance. The significant feature to observe when you are watching the formation of a potential double top is the price level at the lowest point in the valley floor between the two peaks. Once this price level has been penetrated in the decline from the second peak, a sell signal has been given (see the breakout point in Figures 3.10–3.14), and if you own the stock, you should sell it.

Double tops occur because stock owners have good memories. They remember the price they could have gotten had they sold at the first peak. Months, or even a year or so later, when the price returns to that level, they feel that they are being given a second chance to sell at the historical top price, and many of them offer their shares for sale. When the sellers become too anxious and offer more shares than the buyers want, the price is driven down again, because the supply exceeds the demand.

Double-Top Identification Exercise

Review Figures 3E.5–3E.8. Decide whether the price action of each stock shows a double top. If you decide a price pattern shows a double top, check the *yes* response in the figure. If you decide the price pattern does not show a double top, check the *no* response. After indicating your answers, turn to Appendix A, and check your responses.

TRIPLE-TOP FORMATIONS

*Break through =
intermed/long term decline*

Triple-top formations are close relatives of double-top formations. The three tops can be equidistant from each other, or the distance can vary. Any of the tops can be slightly higher or lower than the others (see Figures 3.15–3.17)

After a double top has been formed, a triple top develops when the buyers become anxious as the price declines from the second peak. They start to bid the price back up toward the level of the previous peaks. When the holders of the stock see what may be their final chance to sell at peak prices, they become

Figure 3.10

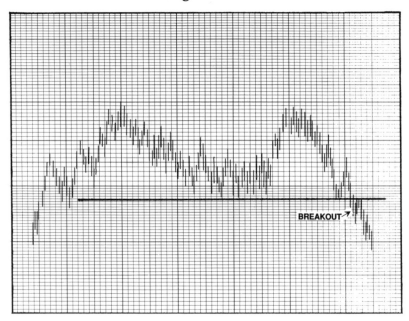

Figure 3.11

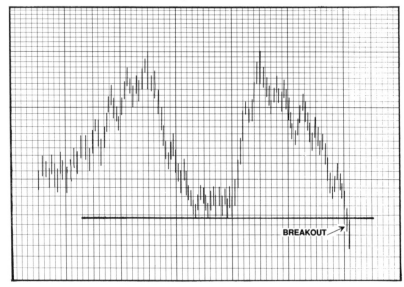

Figures 3.12–3.14

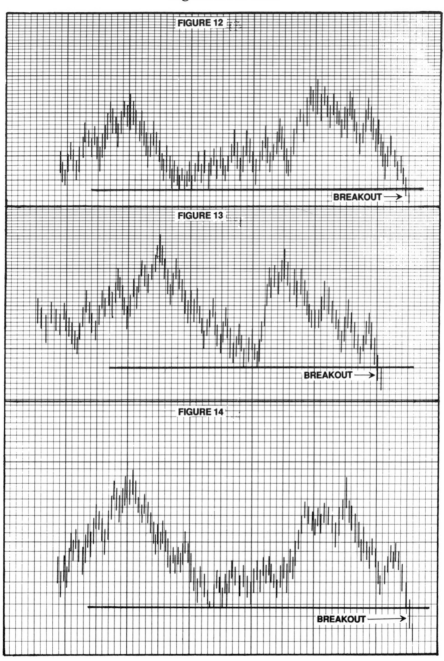

Figure 3E.5

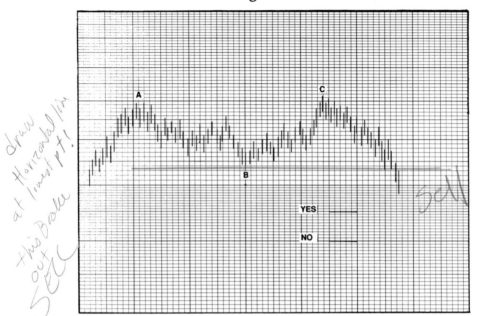

draw
Horizontal line
at lowest pt!
this Broke
out
Sell

Sell

YES _____
NO _____

Figure 3E.6

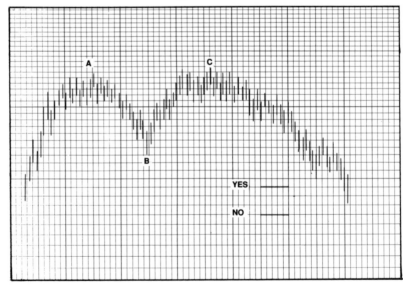

YES _____
NO _____

Figure 3E.7

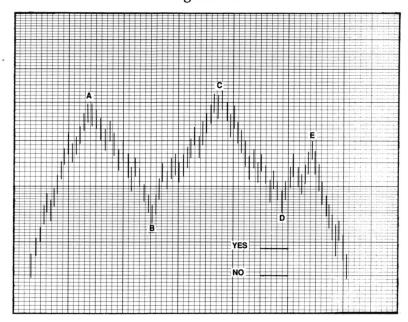

Figure 3E.8

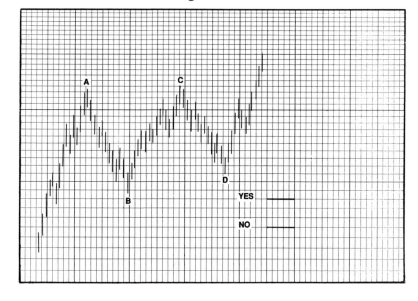

Figures 3.15–3.17
SOME SAMPLES OF TRIPLE TOPS

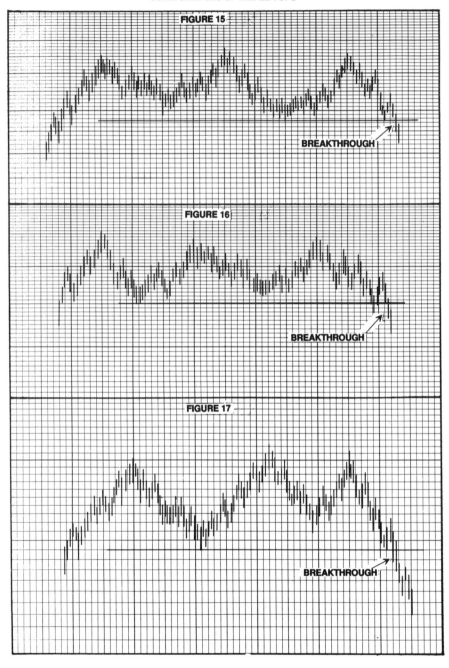

anxious to sell. If too many of them decide to sell, the price is driven down again. When the lower of the two valley-level prices has been penetrated by 5 percent or more (at the close of business), a sell signal has been given, and the price of the stock will usually go into an intermediate or long-term decline.

Triple-Top Identification Exercise

Review Figures 3E.9–3E.12. Decide whether the price action of each stock shows a triple top. If the pattern shows a triple top, check the *yes* response in the chart. If the price pattern does not show a triple top, check the *no* response. After indicating your answers, turn to Appendix A, and check your responses.

ROUNDING-TOP FORMATION

A *rounding-top formation* is a gradual curve which reverses an upward trend and converts it into a downtrend. This gradual reversal usually occurs over a period of several months or longer. The reversal curve may be constructed of relatively small price changes or from large price fluctuations.

A rounding top represents a long struggle between the demand for and the supply of a stock. In the beginning, the demand for the stock is stronger because the buyers are more anxious than the sellers. Gradually, the buyers become less anxious at the higher prices, and the sellers become more anxious until a relative balance in the demand and supply develops. This balance persists for some time, until the sellers start to get more anxious than the buyers. As the sellers' level of anxiety increases, the downward portion of the curve begins to develop. At the right end of the curve, the fears of the sellers have overcome the hopes of the buyers, and a downtrend line can be drawn over the frequent small tops that appear in this type of price pattern (see Figures 3.18 and 3.19).

The significance of a rounding top is usually relative to the length of time it takes to complete itself. A rounding top that is completed in a couple of months will usually be less significant than one that takes a much longer time to complete.

Rounding-Top Identification Exercise

Review Figures 3E.13–3E.18. Decide whether the price action of each stock shows a rounding top. If the price pattern shows a rounding top, check the *yes* response in the chart. If the price pattern does not show a rounding top, check the *no* response. After indicating your answers, turn to Appendix A, and check your responses.

Figure 3E.9

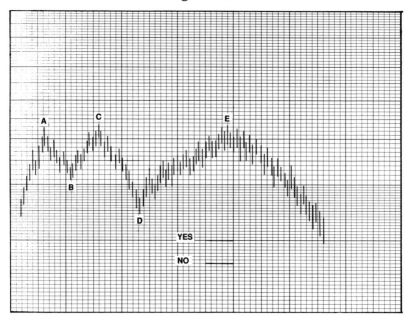

Figure 3E.10

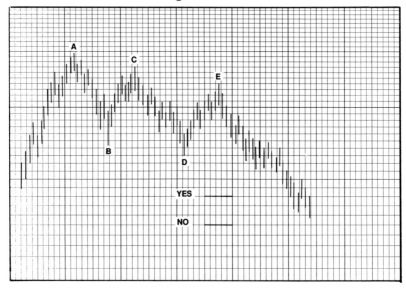

Figure 3E.11

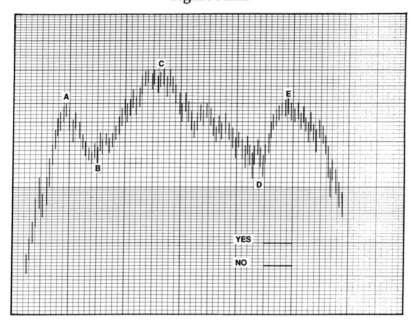

Figure 3E.12

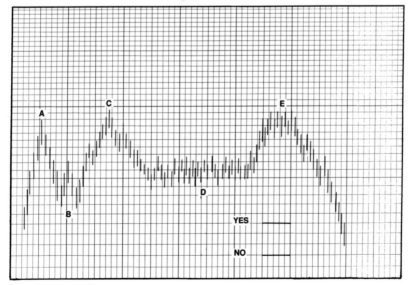

Figure 3.18

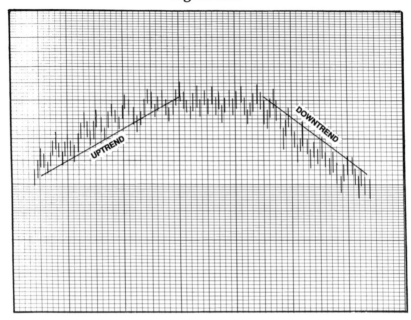

Figure 3.19

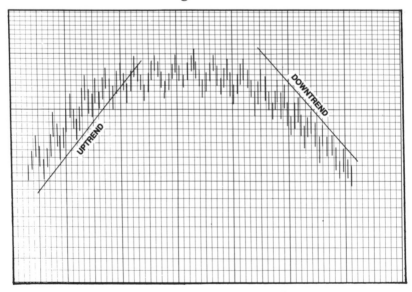

Figure 3E.13

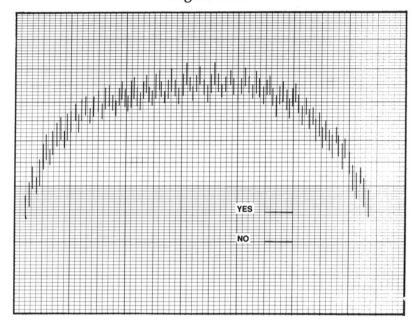

Figure 3E.14

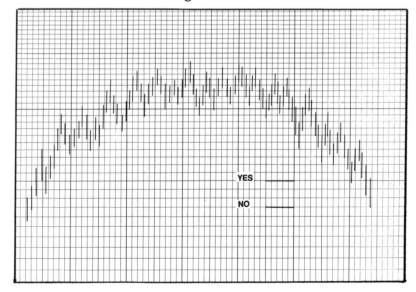

Figure 3E.15

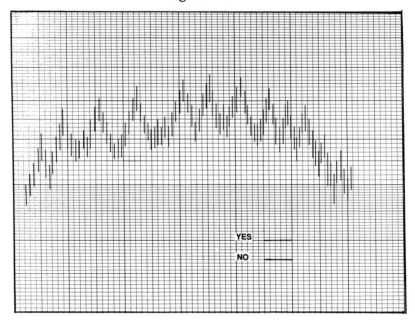

Figure 3E.16

Double Top

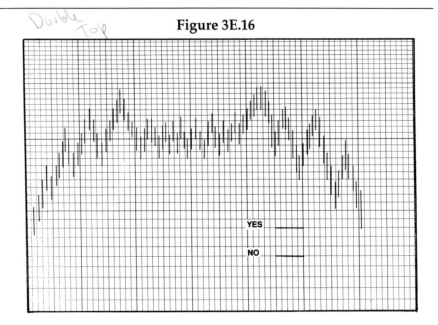

Figure 3E.17

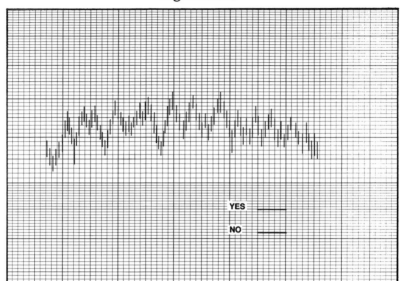

YES _____

NO _____

Figure 3E.18

uptrend changes directly to down trend

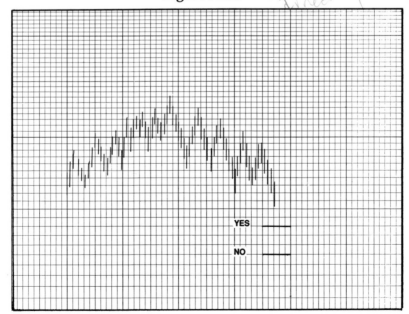

YES _____

NO _____

DESCENDING-TRIANGLE FORMATION

A *descending-triangle formation* develops when a downward slanting line can be drawn through two or more suceeding price peaks and a horizontal line can be drawn through the bottom of two or more intervening price dips (see Figure 3.20). Point B must be lower than point A, and point C must be lower than point B. Points D and E, however, must be at approximately the same price level.

A descending triangle can develop in several weeks or several months. At some point before reaching the apex of the triangle, the price will usually break down through the floor of the triangle. When the price does this and closes 5 percent or more below the bottom line, a sell signal has been given. This penetration will often be accompanied by an increase in sales volume.

If the price does not make a definite penetration of the bottom line as in Figure 3.20, but instead goes out through the apex as in Figure 3.21, the formation loses its significance.

The sales volume tends to diminish as the price works its way into the triangle. Once the price has broken down through the floor of the triangle, the sales volume usually increases—especially if the descent is steep.

Think of a descending triangle as an unequal struggle between sellers who are becoming more and more fearful, and buyers who feel that the shares are a bargain at a particular price level. As it turns out, the buyers prove to be overly optimistic and the sellers' fears are confirmed when the price breaks through the floor of the triangle.

Descending-Triangle Identification Exercise

Review 3E.19–3E.22. Decide whether the price action of each stock shows a descending triangle. If the price pattern shows a descending triangle, check the *yes* response in the chart. If the price pattern does not show a descending triangle, check the *no* response. After indicating your answers, turn to Appendix A, and check your responses.

CONCLUSIONS

1. A reversal formation often provides the clue that an uptrend is ending and the sale of the stock is advisable.

2. Recognizing reversal formations is thus important to profitable operations in the market since knowing when to sell is just as important as knowing what to buy.

Figure 3.20

Figure 3.21

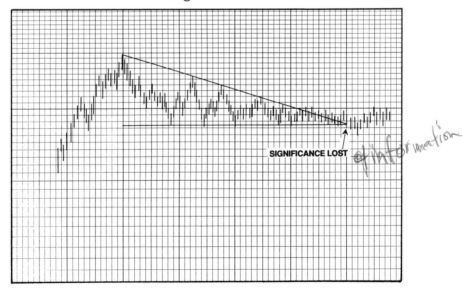

Figure 3E.19

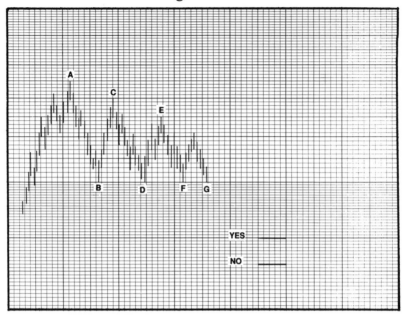

Figure 3E.20

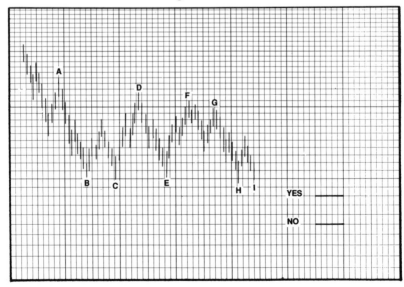

Figure 3E.21

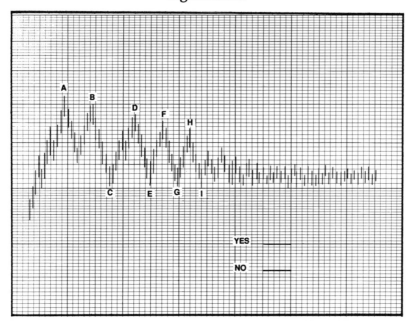

Figure 3E.22

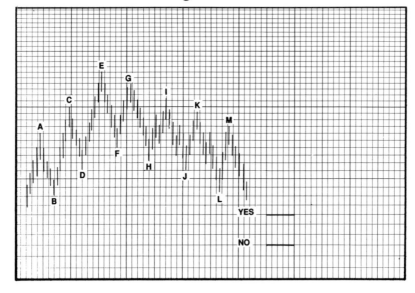

Chapter Four

DOWNTRENDS

Staying out of stocks in downtrends is a key to success in the market. Some stocks go directly into a downtrend from an uptrend. In such cases, you must identify this quick change of direction so that any profits can be salvaged. This is especially important because stocks tend to fall faster than they rise.

When the charted price of a stock shows that successive highs are lower than preceding highs, the stock is said to be in a *downtrend* (see Figure 4.1). In Figure 4.1, point B is lower than point A, and point C is lower than point B.

The downtrend was established as soon as we could draw the downtrend line from A to B. Point C confirms the downtrend as long as it does not penetrate the line before turning downward. When any subsequent top occurs at, near, or below this line, the downtrend is reconfirmed. In many cases the subsequent tops will not even come near the line because downward moves tend to accelerate as they proceed (see Figure 4.2).

Once established, the downtrend indicates that for the time being, the forces of supply (and the fears of the sellers) are stronger than the forces of demand (and the hopes of the buyers). As long as this imbalance continues, the downtrend will remain intact.

When the imbalance is eventually reversed, the downtrend will be broken. Downtrends can be broken right after they become established, or they can continue for months.

The end of a downtrend is signaled by the upward penetration of the downtrend line. To be valid, this penetration should extend by 5 percent of the price at that point. If the penetration occurs at the price level of $20 per share, a closing price of $21 per share would represent a valid breakout from the downtrend line (see Figure 4.3).

POINTS TO REMEMBER

1. Once established, a downward price movement may continue for several weeks, months, or longer.

2. By identifying downtrends and selling quickly, you can salvage most of your profits rather than watch them disappear.

Figure 4.1

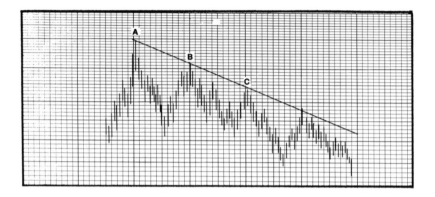

Figure 4.2

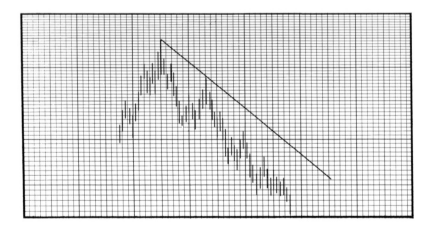

Figure 4.3

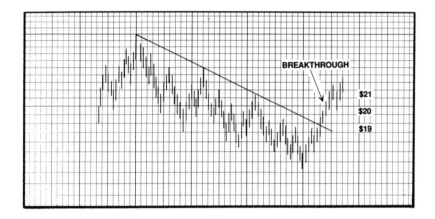

DOWNTREND IDENTIFICATION EXERCISE

Review Figures 4E.1–4E.4. Decide whether the price trend is moving downward. If it is, check the *yes* response in the chart. If not, check the *no* response. After indicating your answers, turn to Appendix A, and check your responses.

Figures 4E.1–4E.4

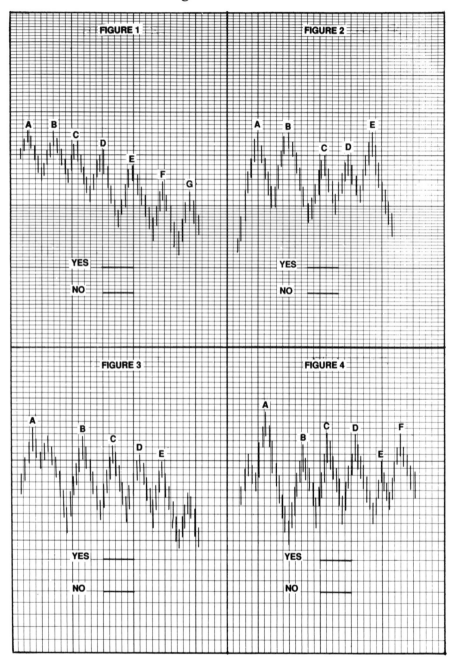

Chapter Five

REVERSAL FORMATIONS AT BOTTOMS

After the price of a stock has declined for a long time, the outlook for the company may take a turn for the better. As this more promising prospect becomes evident to investors, they begin to develop a more positive attitude toward the company. This changing attitude is reflected in the price of the stock as it forms a variety of bottoming-out patterns. These reversal formations at bottoms are described in this chapter.

Before we discuss these reversal formations, consider the situation in which a downtrend in price changes directly into an uptrend (see Figures 5.1 and 5.2). Figure 5.1 is representative of what happens when there is an unexpected announcement of good news. Figure 5.2 shows a common set of price moves. A downtrend tends to accelerate, as shown here. Toward the end of the decline, the price often appears to be on a one-way path to the basement. As the panic increases among sellers, they wind up dumping their shares on the market at whatever price they can get. Finally, the turning point is reached because the stock has been drastically oversold, and bargain hunters move in to pick up the shares at very cheap prices. Then the price is suddenly on the rise again, and a new uptrend establishes itself.

INVERTED HEAD-AND-SHOULDERS FORMATIONS

In Chapter 3, we described the head-and-shoulders reversal formations that can occur at the top of a rise in the price of a stock. When this same formation appears to be standing on its head at the bottom of a fall in the price of a stock, it usually serves as a reversal formation. In this case it could be called an inverted head-and-shoulders formation (see Figures 5.3 and 5.4).

The same characteristics apply to this inverted formation as to the upright formation with one major exception. When the breakout occurs from the neckline by 5 percent, it should be accompanied by a large increase in volume, whereas an increase in volume was not necessary to validate the breakout

Figure 5.1

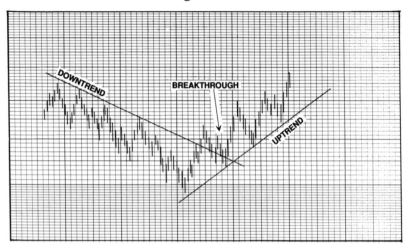

Figure 5.2

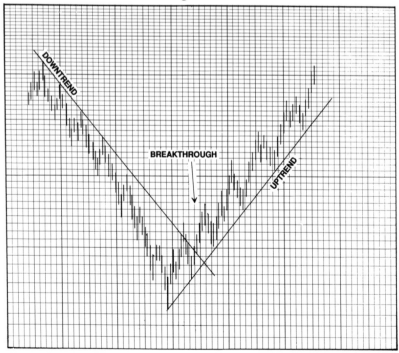

Figure 5.3

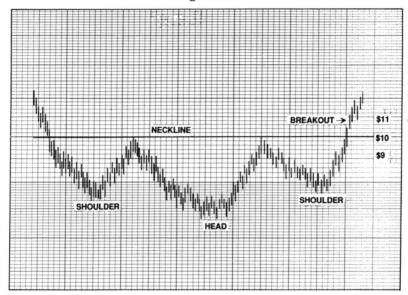

Figure 5.4

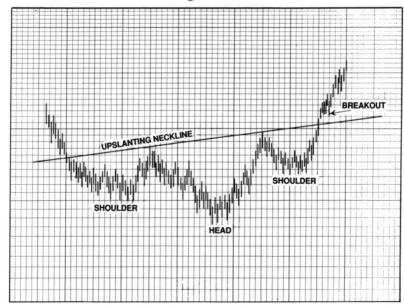

from the upright head and shoulders formation. Once this breakout has occurred, the price of the stock will usually trend upward in an intermediate or long-term move.

Inverted Head-and-Shoulders Identification Exercise

Review Figures 5E.1–5E.4. Decide whether the price action of each stock shows an inverted head-and-shoulders formation. If the price pattern shows an inverted head-and-shoulders formation, check the *yes* response in the chart. If the price pattern does not show an inverted head-and-shoulders formation, check the *no* response. After indicating your answers, turn to Appendix A, and check your responses.

No statement on how fast

ROUNDING BOTTOMS

A rounding bottom is a gentle curve which reverses a downtrend and converts it into an uptrend over a period of several months or longer. This curve represents the gradual change from a supply of stock which is larger than the demand to a period of temporary balance between the supply and the demand, and finally to a situation where the demand is larger than the supply. (See Figures 5.5 and 5.6.)

Because the changes in the supply and demand relationship are so gradual, it is difficult to set up a rule to establish a buying signal at any point in the curve. One way to deal with the ambiguity of the situation is to wait until you notice a sharp increase in the volume as the price moves up the right side of the curve and then decide to make your purchase. A more conservative approach would be to wait until you can draw a definite uptrend line beneath the bottoms before you buy.

Rounding Bottom Identification Exercise

Review Figures 5E.5–5E.8. Decide whether the price action of each stock shows a rounding bottom. If the price pattern shows a rounding bottom, check the *yes* response in the chart. If the price pattern does not show a rounding bottom, check the *no* response. After indicating your answers for all the figures, turn to Appendix A, and check your responses.

Large Δ's more significant price trends than smaller Δ

ASCENDING TRIANGLE FORMATIONS

An *ascending triangle formation* is another means of reversing a downtrend. It develops when an ascending line can be drawn through two or more ascending bottoms and a horizontal line can be drawn through the top of two or more intervening price rises (see Figures 5.7 and 5.8).

Figure 5E.1

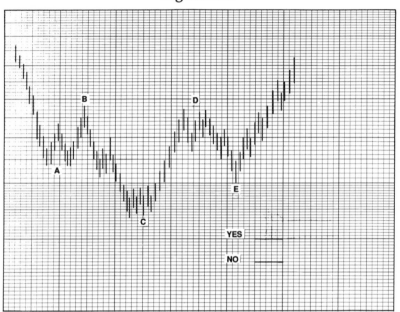

Figure 5E.2

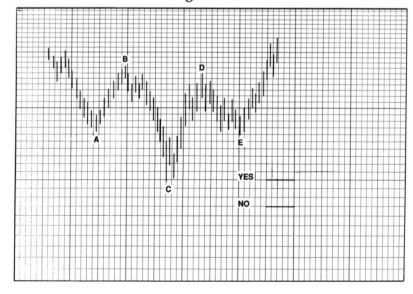

not head& Shoulders
D must be above A

Figure 5E.3

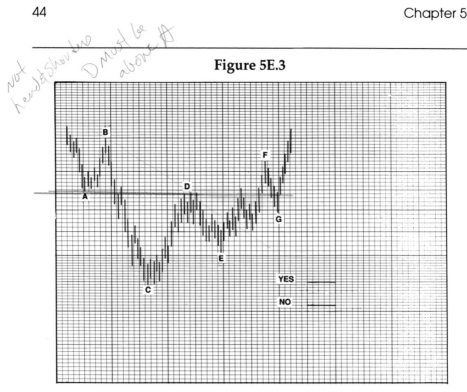

Figure 5E.4

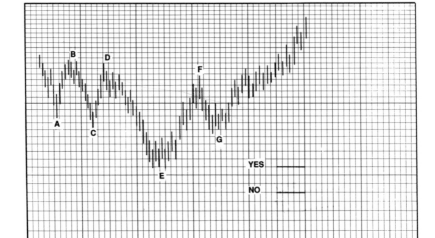

Figure 5.5

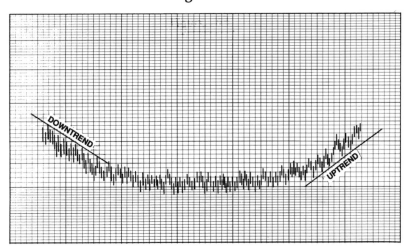

Figure 5.6

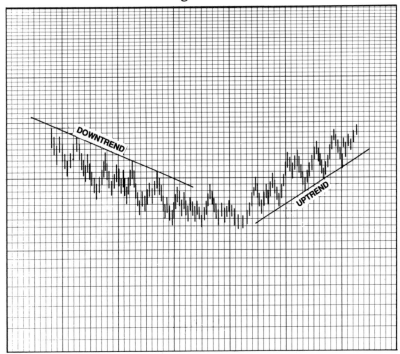

Figure 5E.5

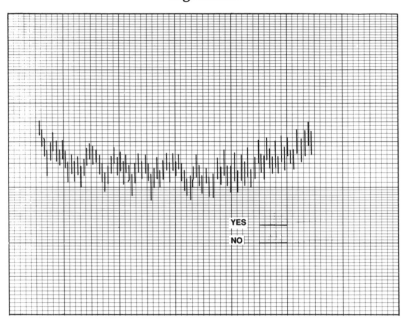

Figure 5E.6

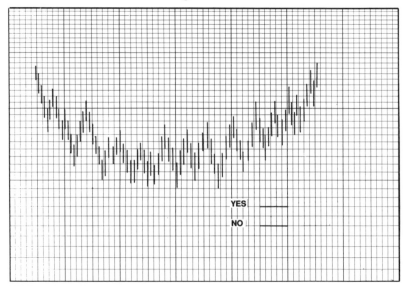

↳ = immediate change

Figure 5E.7 No Rounded Bottom

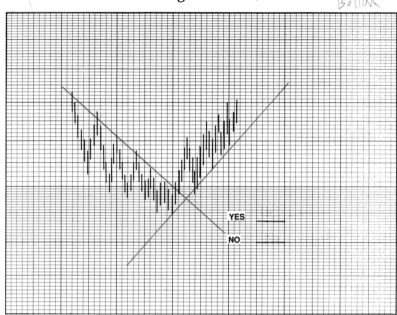

YES _____

NO _____

Figure 5E.8 Not at ↳ this is rounded Bottom

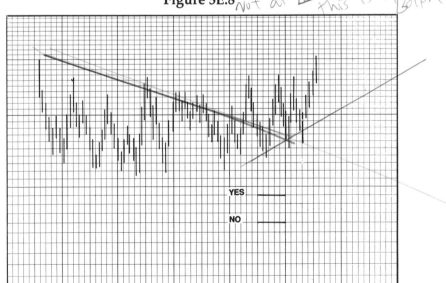

YES _____

NO _____

Figure 5.7

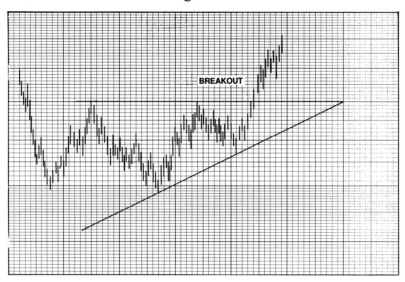

Figure 5.8

An ascending triangle can develop in several weeks, months, or longer. At some point, before reaching the apex, the price should break through the roof of the formation. When the price does this and closes 5 percent or more above the roof line, the buy signal has been given. To be a valid breakthrough, this penetration should be accompanied by a sharp increase in sales volume. As with descending triangles, however, if the price works out through the apex of the triangle, the formation loses its significance (see Figure 5.8).

Picture an ascending triangle as an unequal struggle between buyers who are becoming increasingly hopeful for large profits and sellers who regard the same stock as overpriced at a particular level. As it turns out, the sellers prove to be overly pessimistic, and the buyers' hopes are justified when the price breaks through the roof of the triangle.

Ascending Triangle Identification Exercise

Review the Figures 5E.9–5E.12. Decide whether the price action of each stock shows an ascending triangle. If the price pattern shows an ascending triangle, check the *yes* response in the chart. If the price pattern does not show an ascending triangle, check the *no* response. After indicating your answers, turn to Appendix A, and check your responses.

Bottoms same level Peak in Middle   intermediate to
                                                          long term
Then Breakthrough ## DOUBLE-BOTTOM FORMATIONS   uptrend

A *double-bottom* formation occurs when the price of a stock that has made one bottom and risen for a considerable distance, falls again to approximately the same level as the first bottom, turns up again and then breaks out above the peak between the first and second bottoms (see Figures 5.9 and 5.10).

Double bottoms occur because the potential buyers of a stock that has risen from the first bottom remember the price at which they could have bought the stock at some time in the past. When the price of the stock goes back down to that level, they become eager to buy the stock. When, as a group, they want to buy more shares than are being offered for sale at the second bottom, they begin chasing the stock upward with their offers to buy. If their combined eagerness to buy is great enough, the price advances above the intervening price peak. Such a breakout usually develops into an intermediate or long-term uptrend.

Double-Bottom Identification Exercise

Review the Figures 5E.13–5E.16. Decide whether the price action of each stock shows a double bottom. If it does, check the *yes* response in the chart. If it does not, check the *no* response. After completing this exercise, turn to Appendix A, and check your answers.

Ascending Triangles

Figure 5E.9

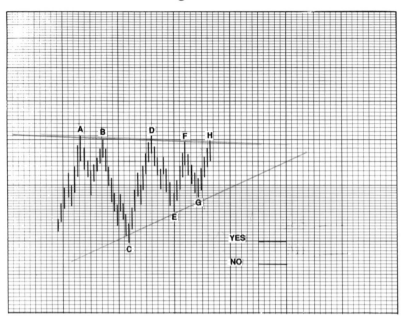

No / Tops are sequentially lower

Figure 5E.10

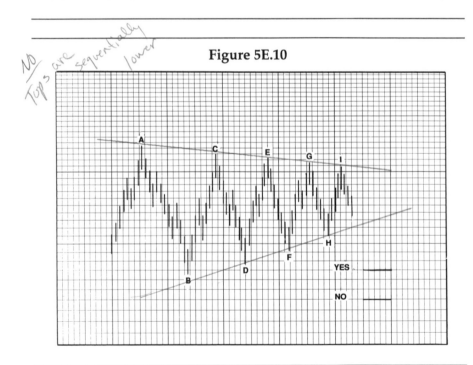

Figure 5E.11

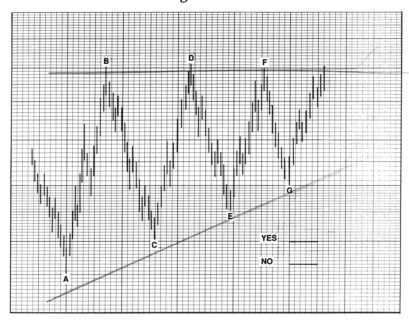

Figure 5E.12

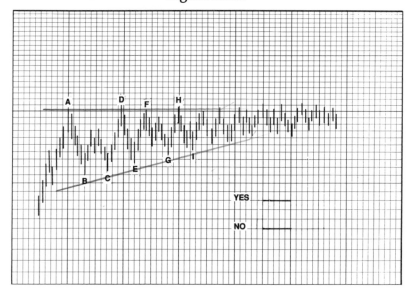

Figure 5.9

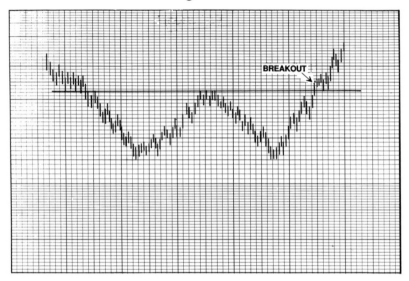

Figure 5.10

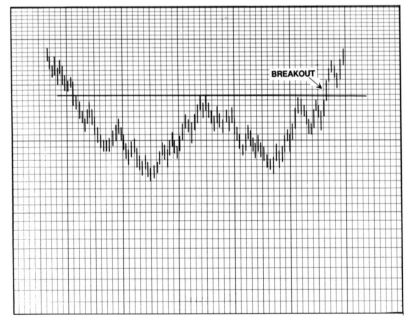

Figure 5E.13

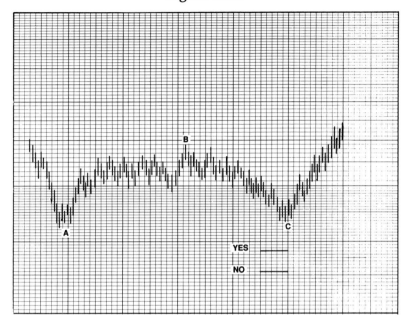

Figure 5E.14

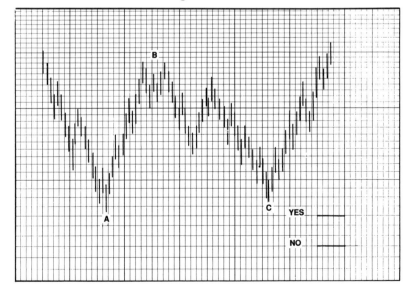

Double Bottom

Figure 5E.15

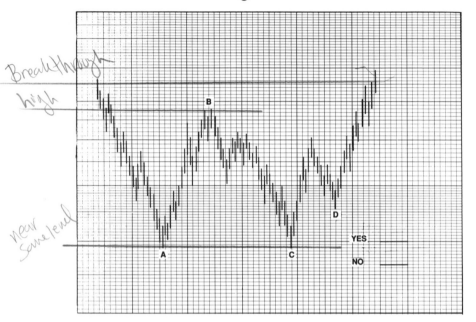

Breakthrough

high

near
Same level

B

A   C   YES

D

NO

Figure 5E.16

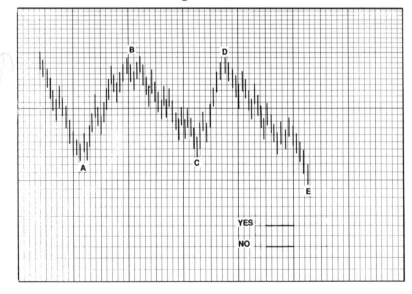

B   D

A   C

E

YES

NO

[handwritten: inter med or long term uptrend)]

TRIPLE-BOTTOM FORMATIONS

A *triple-bottom formation* can occur when the price of a stock fails to surpass the intervening peak mentioned in the preceding section on double bottoms. Instead of rising above the intervening peak the price retreats and goes down to approximately the same level as the two preceding bottoms. Then it starts another rise, and on this try it manages to break out above the higher of the two intervening price peaks (see Figures 5.11 and 5.12).

As the price rises for the third time, the volume generated will usually be greater than that generated in the previous rises. When this occurs, the price of the stock has the potential to develop an intermediate or long-term uptrend.

Triple-Bottom Identification Exercise

Review the Figures 5E.17–5E.20. Decide whether the price action of each stock shows a triple bottom. If it does, check the *yes* response in the chart. If not, check the *no* reponse in the chart. After indicating your answers, turn to Appendix A, and check your responses.

[handwritten: Break out w/ high Vol — SIGNIFICANT PRICE RISE (usually)]

TRADING RANGE BOTTOMS

[handwritten: Rolling stock]

Sometimes after a long decline, a stock will make three or more bottoms at approximately the same price, and make three or more intervening tops at approximately the same price, thus establishing what can be called a *trading range*, within which the price may fluctuate from several months to several years. If the price eventually breaks out to the upside of this range, this formation is then called a *trading range bottom*. If this breakout occurs on a large increase in volume and an uptrend becomes established, a significant price rise usually develops.

POINTS TO REMEMBER

1. A bottom can be made in one day or may take several years to complete.
2. A bottom can be defined only after its completion.
3. Three features are characteristic of significant bottoms:
    -   A breakout to the upside
    -   A large increase in trading volume in conjunction with the breakout
    -   Subsequent establishment of an uptrend

4. The patience to wait for the completion of a bottom before making a purchase will often be rewarded handsomely.

Figure 5.11

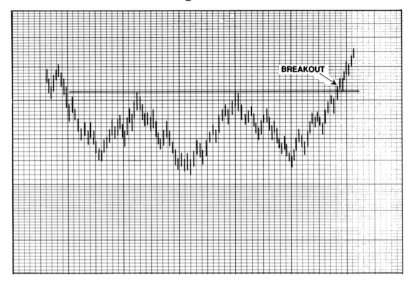

Figure 5.12

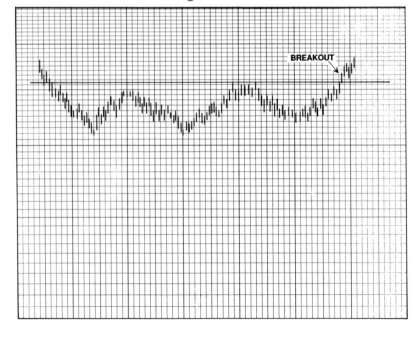

Figure 5E.17

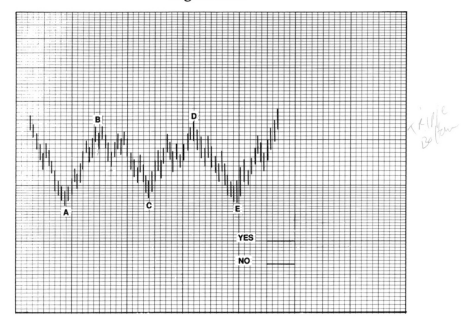

Figure 5E.18

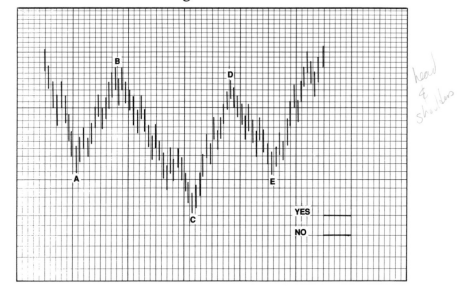

Figure 5E.19
WHICH ARE TRIPLE BOTTOMS?

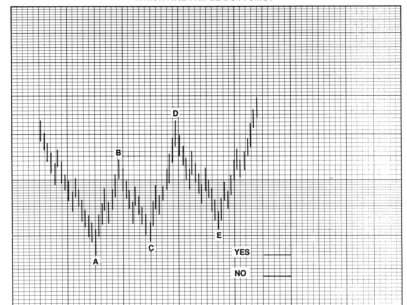

Figure 5E.20

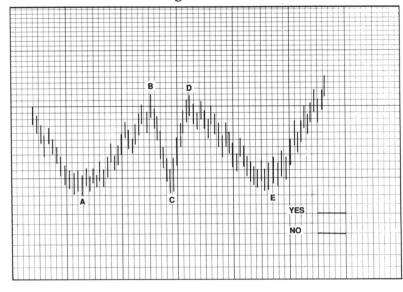

Chapter Six

CONTINUATION AND REVERSAL FORMATIONS

Stock prices do not go anywhere in a straight line. For two steps forward, they often take one step backward. Often they meander or enter into periods of indecision where the forces of supply and demand are pretty much in balance. Whether a stock is going up or down, it may enter into one of these phases at any point and spend some time vacillating before it goes up or down subsequently. This chapter reviews these phases of vacillation and indecision.

SYMMETRICAL TRIANGLES

We have already described the ascending and descending triangles. A symmetrical triangle does not have an upward or downward slant but has a horizontal axis (see Figures 6.1–6.6).

Symmetrical triangles are formed when price fluctuations result in two consecutive descending tops and two consecutive ascending bottoms. Drawing lines through the tops and the bottoms defines the boundaries of indecision.

As the price of the stock works its way out toward the apex of the triangle, the volume tends to diminish. At some point, usually within two or three months, the demand or supply side suddenly overwhelms the opposition and the breakout occurs. The breakout is often accompanied by an increase in volume. When the closing price goes beyond the side of the triangle by 5 percent or more, the breakout has been confirmed.

The symmetrical triangle is called a *continuation formation* because most of the time the breakout will be in the same direction (up or down) as the price was headed prior to the triangle creation. When the price breaks out in the opposite direction, the triangle serves as a *reversal formation* (see Figure 6.5). As with the other triangles, if the price works its way out through the apex, the triangle loses its significance (see Figure 6.6). A symmetrical triangle does not have to be perfectly symmetrical in order to be classed as such. It is only

Figures 6.1–6.6

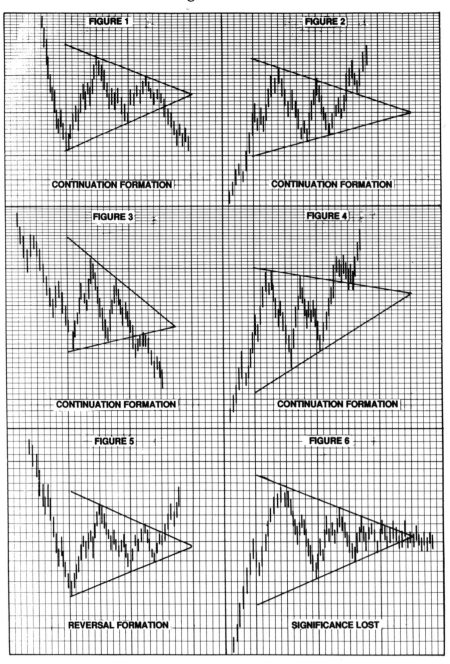

Det of semetrical △

necessary that the bottom line slant upward and the top line slant downward (see Figures 6.3 and 6.4).

While breakouts on the upside should be accompanied by an increase in volume to be reliable, a breakout on the downside does not require an increase in volume to be taken seriously.

Symmetrical Triangle Identification Exercise

Review Figures 6E.1–6E.6. Decide whether the price action of each stock can be described as a symmetrical triangle. If it can, check the *yes* response in the chart. If not, check the *no* response. After indicating your answers, turn to Appendix A, and check your responses.

Rally Stock

RECTANGLES/TRADING RANGES

A *rectangle* (also referred to as a *trading range*) is formed when a line drawn through two or more tops and a line drawn through two or more bottoms are horizontal and parallel lines (see Figures 6.7–6.9). These formations are created when a large group of potential buyers becomes convinced that a stock is a bargain at the price coinciding with the bottom line. When the price gets down to that level, they are anxious to buy. On the other hand, many of the current holders of the stock are convinced that the stock is overpriced when it gets to the upper horizontal line, and they are happy to sell at that level.

This situation results in what may be called a *support level* at the lower price and a *resistance level* at the upper price. The space between these two levels becomes a *trading range*. Often, the difference between the price at the upper level and the price at the lower level is just a few dollars—indicating that the supply and demand for the stock are in relative balance. Eventually (sometimes trading ranges persist for several years) the forces of supply and demand become unbalanced—usually because of a wide-spread rumor or a major news event. If the price then breaks out in the same direction it was moving before it formed the rectangle, the rectangle has served as a continuation formation (see Figures 6.7 and 6.8).

If the price breaks out in the opposite direction, the rectangle has functioned as a reversal formation (see Figure 6.9).

Rectangle/Trading Range Identification Exercise

Review Figures 6E.7–6E.10. Decide whether the price action of each stock shows a rectangle/trading range. If it does, check the *yes* response in the chart. If it doesn't, check the *no* response. After indicating your answers, turn to Appendix A, and check your responses.

Figures 6E.1–6E.4

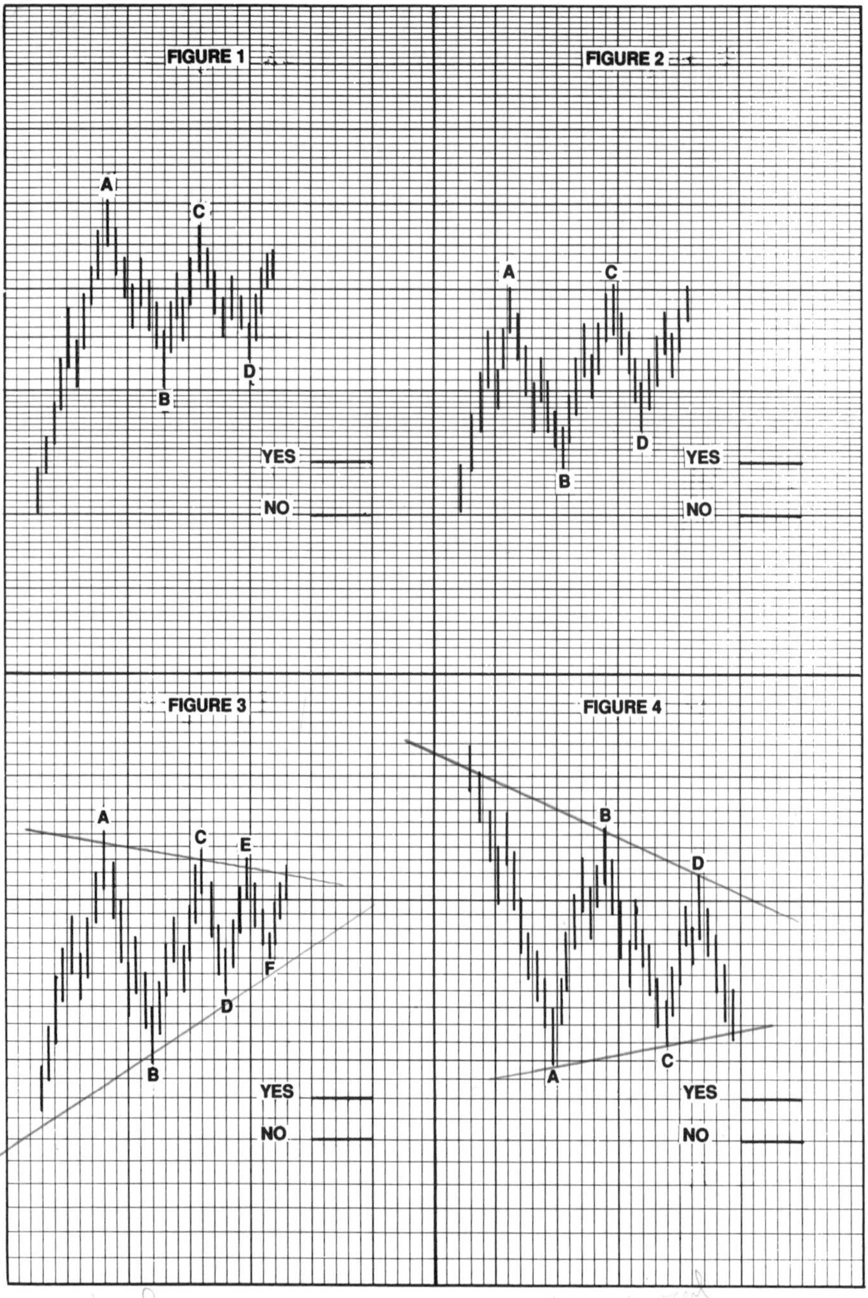

Handwritten annotations:

Semetrical △ (top left)

ascending △ (top right)

FIGURE 1 — points labeled A, C, B, D; YES ___ NO ___

FIGURE 2 — points labeled A, C, B, D; YES ___ NO ___

FIGURE 3 — points labeled A, C, E, B, D, F; YES ___ NO ___

FIGURE 4 — points labeled B, D, A, C; YES ___ NO ___

(left margin, Figure 3): Sharper UP than down Breakout probably UP

Semetrical w/ ↑ Bias (bottom left)

Semetrical w/ ↓ Bias (bottom right)

Figure 6E.5
WHICH ARE SYMMETRICAL TRIANGLES?

Large △ - when Break out comes it should be significant

Semetrical

YES _____

NO _____

Figure 6E.6

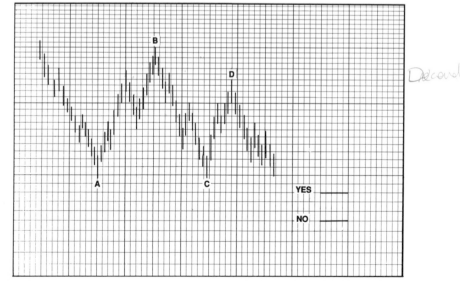

Descending

YES _____

NO _____

Figures 6.7–6.9

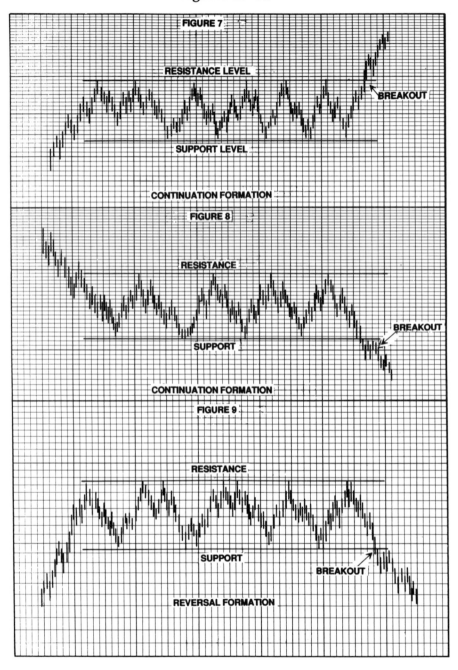

Figure 6E.7

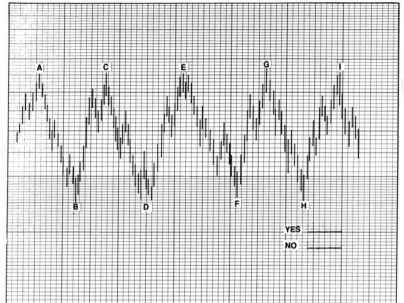

range
(rally)

Figure 6E.8

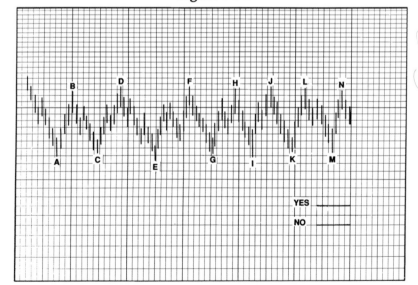

range
(rally)

Figure 6E.9

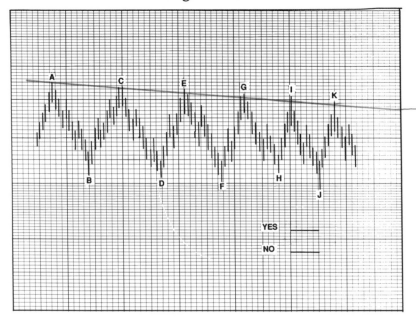

Down trend

Figure 6E.10

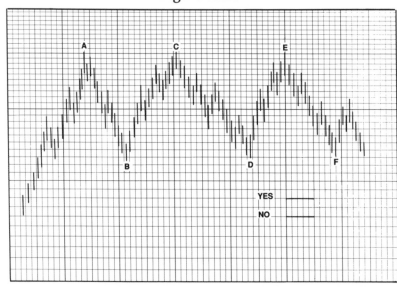

Range (Rolling)

OTHER TRIANGLES AS CONTINUATION FORMATIONS

Descending triangles serve as reversal formations at tops, and ascending triangles serve as reversal formations at bottoms. Both types of triangles can also serve as continuation formations. At any point in a down move, the price action could develop into a descending triangle. In most cases, the price would eventually break through the floor of the triangle and would then have served as a continuation formation. Similarly, in an up move, price action could develop into an ascending triangle, and if a breakout through the roof occurs, the triangle would have served as a continuation formation.

POINTS TO REMEMBER

1. Continuation formations are periods of relative balance between the forces of supply and demand.

2. If you own a stock that has entered a continuation formation after an uptrend, you may want to hold it patiently, because the price usually breaks out on the upside.

3. If the period of indecision turns out to be a reversal formation instead of a continuation formation, it is time to sell.

Chapter Seven
ANALYZING VOLUME

Chapters 2 through 6 concentrated on price movements and patterns. This chapter focuses on the volume of trading and how it relates to these price movements and patterns.

We present examples of the following concepts and discuss how an investor can use these concepts to make profitable buy, hold, and sell decisions:

1. The volume of trading usually increases and remains higher than average during an uptrend.

2. The volume of trading usually increases as the price breaks out to the *side* upside of a formation or pattern, and a large increase in volume provides a strong buy signal.

3. Volume is usually lower than average during a downtrend.

4. A price breakout to the downside of a formation or pattern gives a sell signal whether the volume of trading increases or not.

5. Volume usually decreases inside triangles.

VOLUME CHARACTERISTICS IN UPTRENDS

When a stock price goes into and maintains an uptrend, the average daily trading volume usually rises because a rising price attracts more and more investors who want to get into a winning situation. Figures 7.1–7.4 are examples of how trading volume expands to initiate and sustain an uptrend.

The three volume characteristics of uptrends illustrated in Figures 7.1–7.4 are these:

- The volume of trading increased as the uptrend started.

- The volume fluctuated as the uptrend continued.

- In spite of the fluctuations, the volume of trading was generally higher than average during the uptrend.

Figure 7.1
DOWNTREND CHANGES TO UPTREND

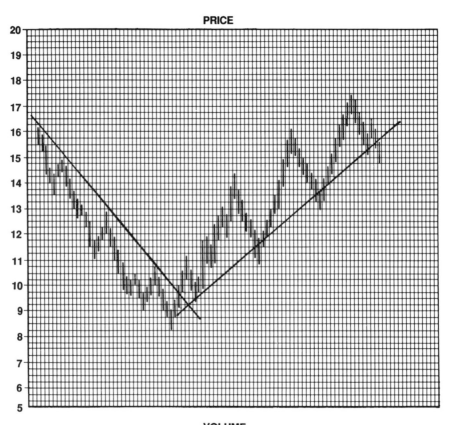

PRICE

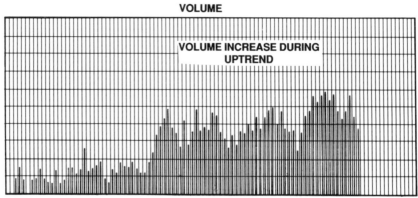

VOLUME

VOLUME INCREASE DURING UPTREND

Figure 7.2
RESISTANCE LEVEL BROKEN BY UPTREND

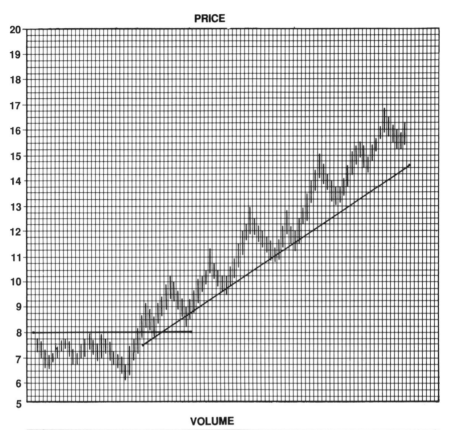

PRICE

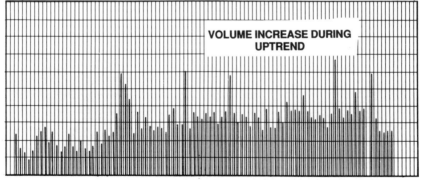

VOLUME

VOLUME INCREASE DURING UPTREND

Figure 7.3
HEAD-AND-SHOULDERS BOTTOM CHANGES TO UPTREND

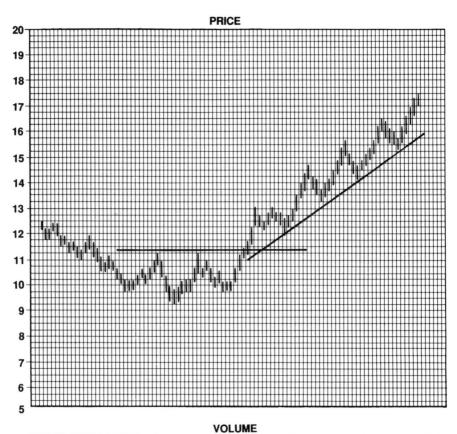

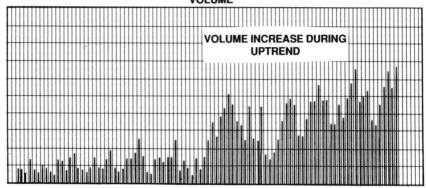

Figure 7.4
RESISTANCE LEVEL BROKEN BY UPTREND

PRICE

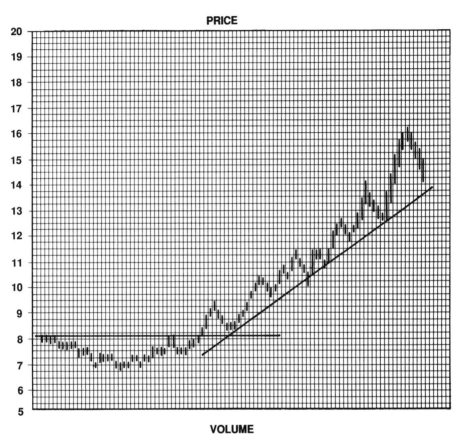

VOLUME

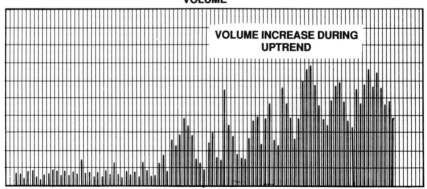

VOLUME INCREASE DURING UPTREND

You can use this information to help make decisions to buy, hold, or sell a stock. If you are thinking about purchasing a particular stock and it is just establishing an uptrend, you should not buy unless you see the volume increase as it starts its initial rise. When the volume has increased for several days, or has been exceptionally high for one or two days, there is a higher probability that the uptrend can sustain itself. On the other hand, if the start of the uptrend is not accompanied by increased volume, there is a lower probability that the uptrend can be sustained. Once you make the purchase, you should hold onto the stock no matter how the volume fluctuates—as long as the price remains above the uptrend line. The time to sell is when the price of the stock declines below the uptrend line by 5 percent or more. When this happens, you should sell whether the volume increases, decreases, or stays the same at the breakout.

Volume Characteristics of Upside Breakouts

An increase in trading volume serves to confirm the significance of an upside breakout from a price pattern or formation. The larger the increase in volume, the greater is the price rise potential signified by the breakout. Figures 7.5–7.8 are examples of how trading volume expands in conjunction with an upside breakout above a boundary line, trend line, or neckline.

The best time to buy a stock is just after it has made a high-volume breakout to the upside of a bottom formation. Figures 7.5–7.8 show these types of breakouts and how they are usually followed by extended price uptrends of intermediate or long-term duration. This combination of an upside price breakout and a large increase in volume represents a strong buy signal. This type of signal presents the opportunity to buy at a lower price than if you waited for an uptrend to become established, so the potential profit is larger. Once the uptrend line becomes established, you should hold the stock until the price uptrend line is penetrated by 5 percent.

ELONGATED TRADING RANGE

Another type of price-and-volume relationship occurs within an elongated trading range. After a stock has dropped to a low price, it may trade for a long time (up to several years) in an elongated trading range. When this occurs, the trading volume is usually very low because most investors are not interested in stocks that are in the doldrums. However, if the price should some day break out above the resistance level accompanied by a large increase in trading volume, it represents one of the very best buying opportunities for a large potential profit.

Figures 7.9–7.12 are examples of elongated trading ranges.

Figure 7.5
HEAD-AND-SHOULDERS BOTTOM CHANGES TO UPTREND

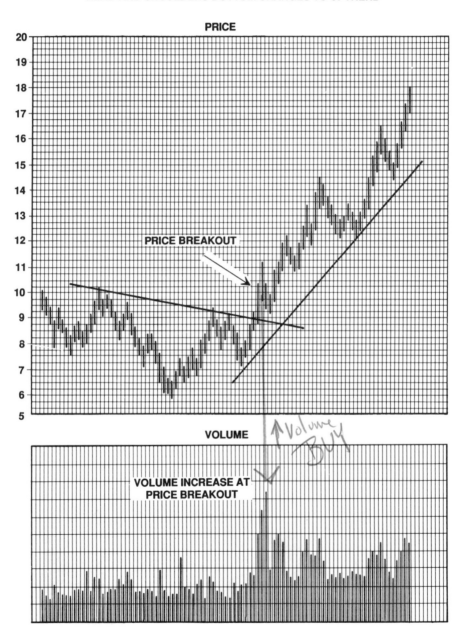

PRICE

PRICE BREAKOUT

VOLUME

VOLUME INCREASE AT
PRICE BREAKOUT

Figure 7.6
DOUBLE BOTTOM CHANGES TO UPTREND

PRICE

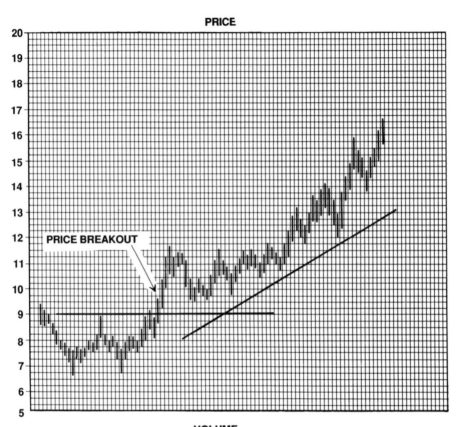

VOLUME

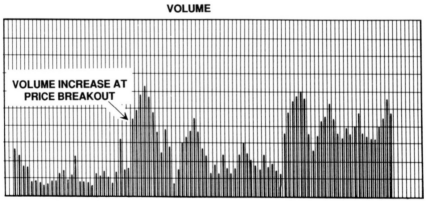

Figure 7.7
TRIPLE BOTTOM CHANGES TO UPTREND

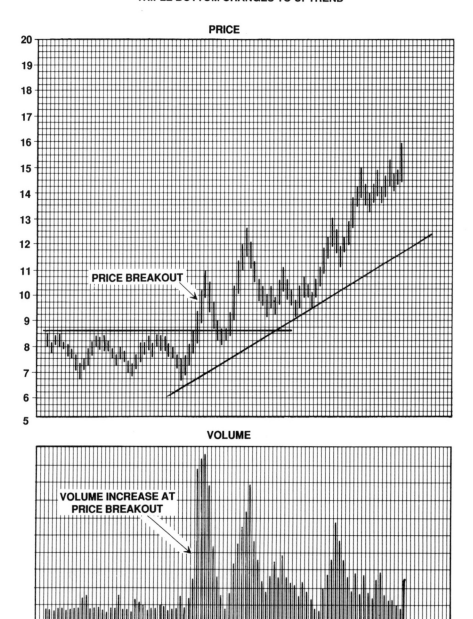

Figure 7.8
DOWNTREND CHANGES TO UPTREND

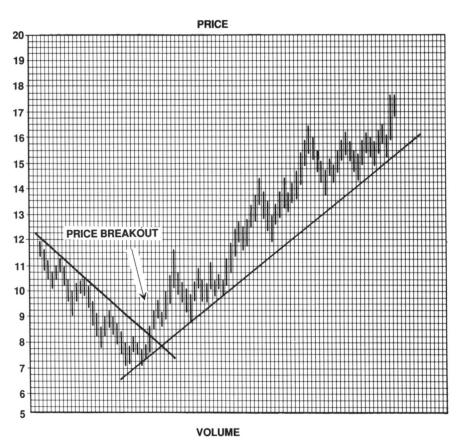

PRICE

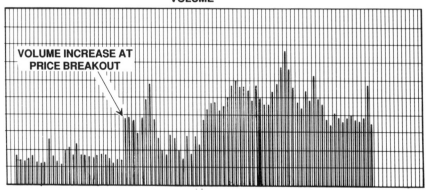

VOLUME

Figure 7.9
ELONGATED TRADING RANGE

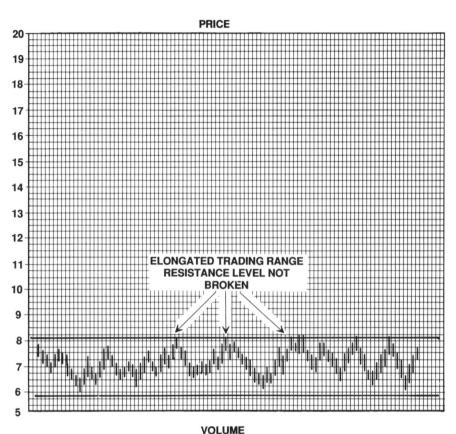

PRICE

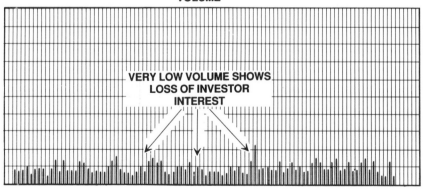

VOLUME

Figure 7.10
ELONGATED TRADING RANGE

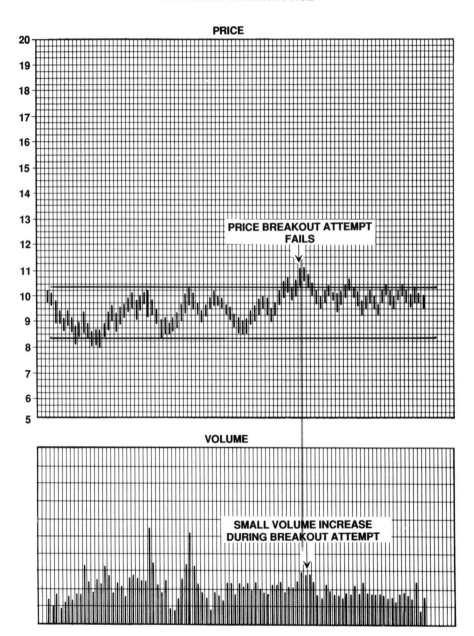

Figure 7.11
ELONGATED TRADING RANGE CHANGES TO UPTREND

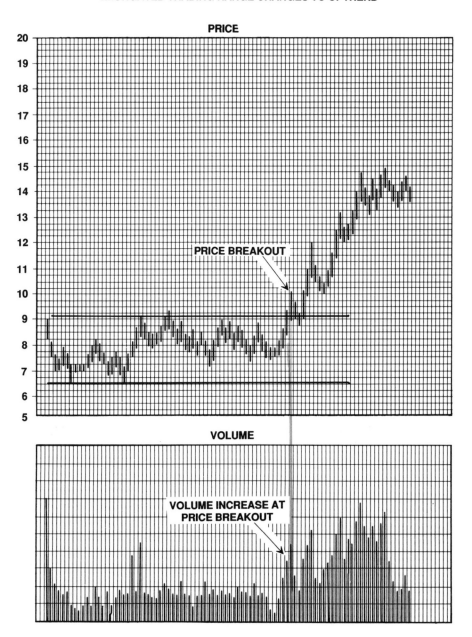

Figure 7.12
ELONGATED TRADING RANGE CHANGES TO UPTREND

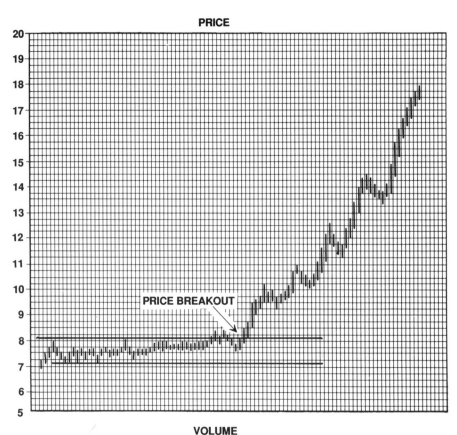

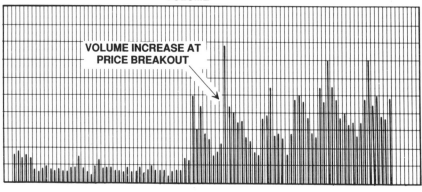

In Figure 7.9, the price of the stock was not able to break out above the resistance level of $8 per share. You might be tempted to buy this stock at the support level of $6 per share, but it would not be advisable for two reasons:

- The price of the stock could continue trading in that range for years, so you would be wasting a lot of time. *No- Rolling Stock - Trade w/ in Range*
- The price might break out to the downside of the trading range, putting you in a potential losing situation. *TRUE - Use Stop/oss*

In Figure 7.10, the price of the stock did break out above the $10-per-share resistance level and reached $11 per share temporarily. However, the volume of trading did not increase significantly, so you should not buy this stock either.

In Figures 7.11 and 7.12, the price of the stock broke out above the $8 and $9 per share resistance levels respectively, and the volume of trading increased significantly. This simultaneous price and volume increase is one of the best buying opportunities.

VOLUME CHARACTERISTICS OF DOWNTRENDS

When a stock price goes into and maintains a downtrend, the average daily trading volume usually declines. This occurs because potential buyers tend to lose interest in a stock when they see that its price is declining. A rising price is usually accompanied by increased volume, but the price can fall without a rise in volume if potential buyers lose interest. However, higher volume can also accompany a falling stock price; this situation occurs when there is some negative information about the company that causes many of the stockholders to decide to sell. Figures 7.13–7.17 are examples of the differences in trading volume that tend to accompany downtrends.

Each of Figures 7.13–7.17 illustrates an extended decline from the peak price. In Figures 7.13 and 7.14, the average trading volume declines during the downtrend in price. In Figures 7.15 and 7.16, the average daily trading volume increases while the downtrend continues. In Figure 7.17, a downtrend develops from a rounding top; during this downtrend no significant change in the daily trading volume occurs.

Taken as a group these five examples illustrate that extended downtrends can occur while the average daily trading volume decreases, increases, or remains about the same. If you are holding a stock that starts into a downtrend, you should sell it as soon as the downtrend becomes established because there is no reliable method to predict the extent of the price decline from the volume of trading that accompanies it.

Figure 7.13
UPTREND CHANGES TO DOWNTREND

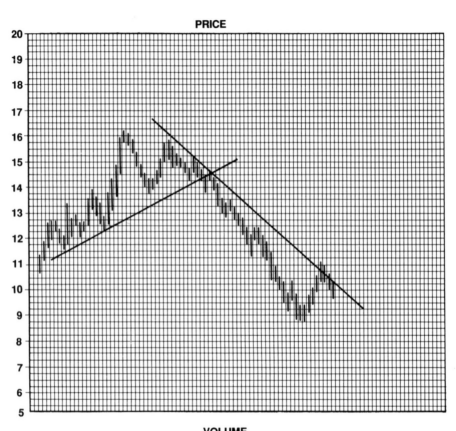

PRICE

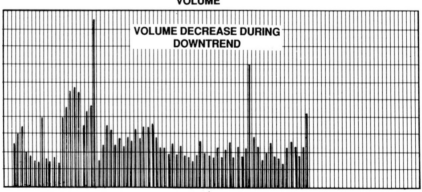

VOLUME

VOLUME DECREASE DURING
DOWNTREND

Figure 7.14
SYMMETRICAL TRIANGLE CHANGES TO DOWNTREND

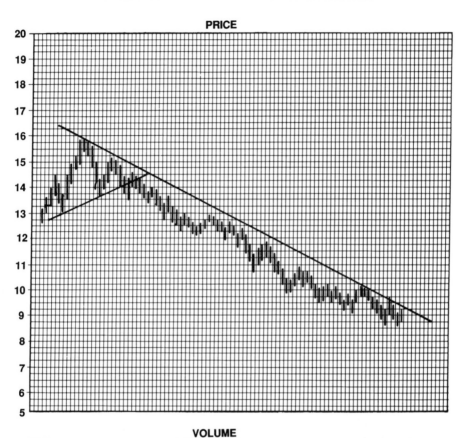

PRICE

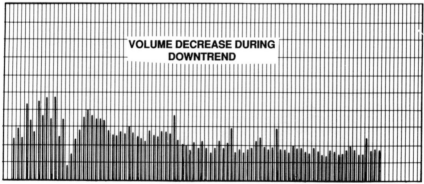

VOLUME

VOLUME DECREASE DURING
DOWNTREND

Figure 7.15
UPTREND CHANGES TO DOWNTREND

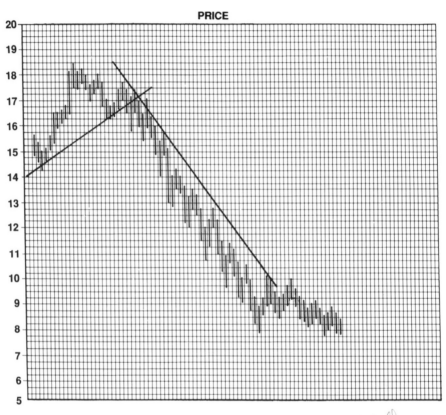

PRICE

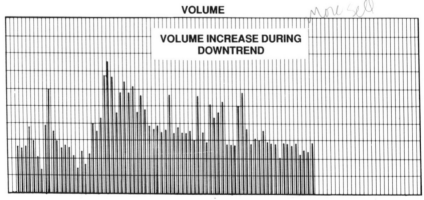

VOLUME

VOLUME INCREASE DURING DOWNTREND

Figure 7.16
DESCENDING TRIANGLE CHANGES TO DOWNTREND

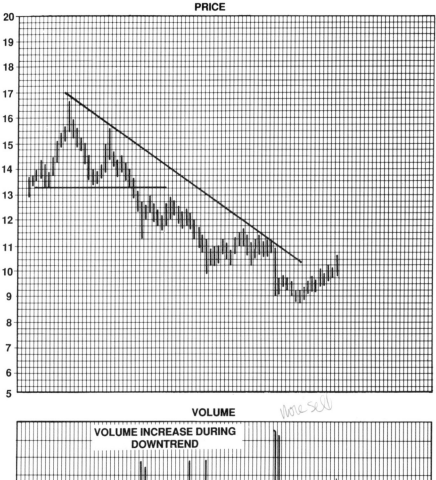

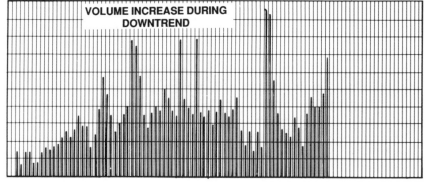

Figure 7.17
ROUNDING TOP CHANGES TO DOWNTREND

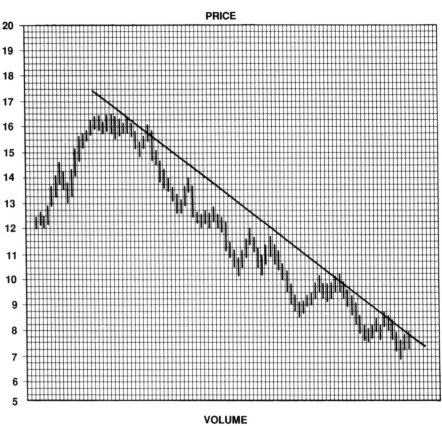

PRICE

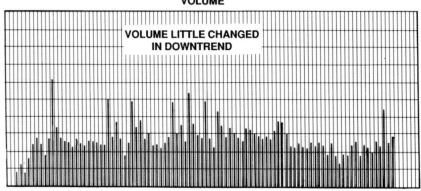

VOLUME

**VOLUME LITTLE CHANGED
IN DOWNTREND**

Volume Characteristics of Downside Breakouts

If you are holding a stock, another danger signal to watch for is the downside breakout below a price pattern or formation. These downside breakouts provide a sell signal, regardless of the accompanying volume of trading. The downside breakouts to watch out for are those from head-and-shoulders formations, double-top formations, triple tops, triangles, and rectangles. Figures 7.18–7.23 show the differences in trading volume that accompany these breakouts.

Figures 7.18–7.23 show that while volume at breakouts varies, the result is generally the same: an extended, intermediate, or long- term decline in price. If you own a stock making such a price breakout to the downside, you should sell it, regardless of the volume of trading. However, there are rare occasions when the subsequent price decline is of short-term duration, but you should not hold on to a stock in the hope that this will happen.

VOLUME CHARACTERISTICS WITHIN TRIANGLES

Volume usually declines as the price of a stock forms a triangle. These patterns represent periods of indecision. Because investors do not like the uncertainty of the situation, many prefer to withdraw to the sidelines to wait and see who will win the struggle—the buyers or the sellers. Figures 7.24–7.26 are examples of the volume of trading within triangles.

Figures 7.24–7.26 show that there can be three different resolutions to this type of buyer-versus-seller struggle:

- The buyers can win and the price breakout is to the upside.

- The sellers can win and the price breaks out to the downside.

- The result can be a draw, and the price goes out through the apex of the triangle.

How can you deal with each of these situations? If you are thinking about buying, you should do so only if the breakout is to the upside and there is a large increase in trading volume. If you already own the stock, you should sell if the breakout is to the downside. If the price works its way out through the apex of the triangle, you should be patient and wait for something more definitive to happen.

COMPARING VOLUME DIMENSIONS

In addition to published price-and-volume charts, another good source of information on trading volume is *The Wall Street Journal*. Once a month (between the 20th and the 25th of the month), *The Wall Street Journal* prints statistics on the average daily trading volume for hundreds of stocks; it is presented along with the short interest figures for the month. By checking

Figure 7.18
HEAD-AND-SHOULDERS TOP CHANGES TO DOWNTREND

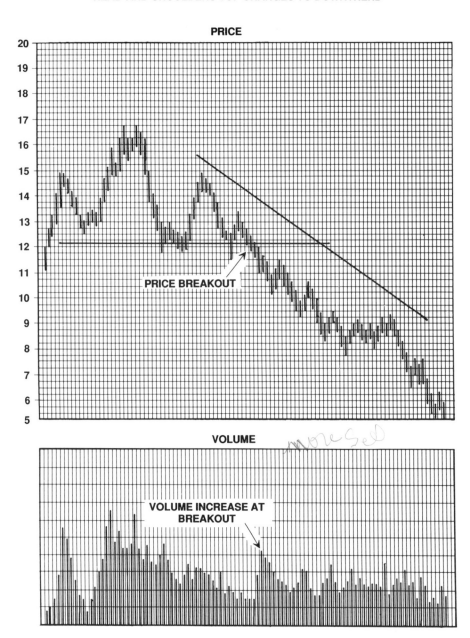

Figure 7.19
DOUBLE TOP CHANGES TO DOWNTREND

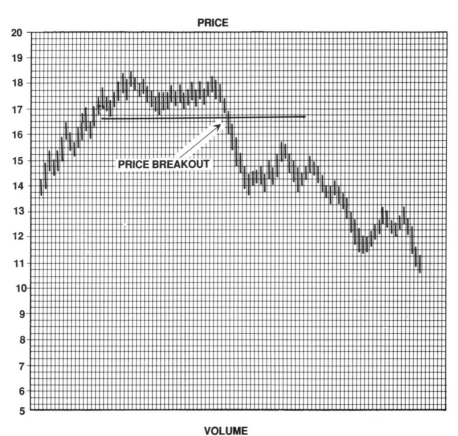

PRICE

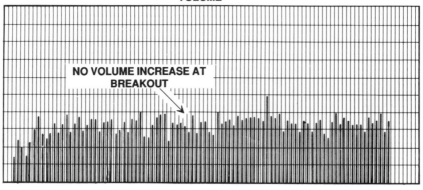

VOLUME

Figure 7.20
TRIPLE TOP CHANGES TO DOWNTREND

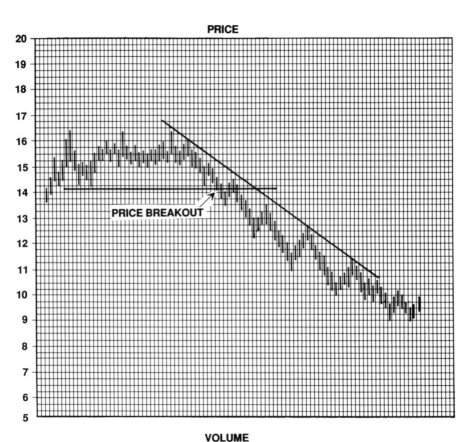

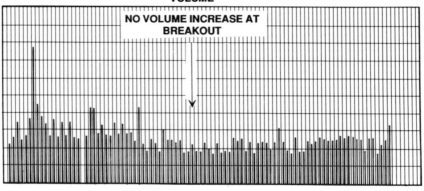

Figure 7.21
DESCENDING TRIANGLE CHANGES TO DOWNTREND

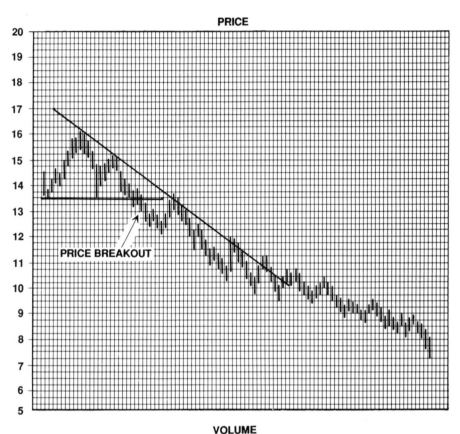

PRICE

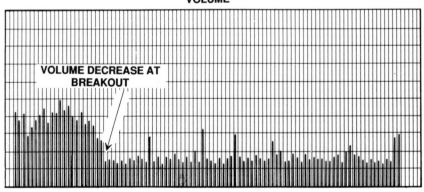

VOLUME

Figure 7.22
SYMMETRICAL TRIANGLE CHANGES TO DOWNTREND

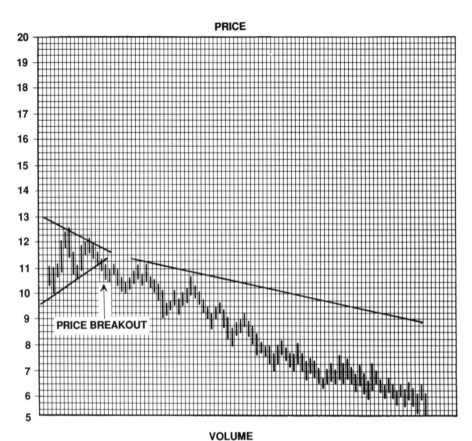

PRICE

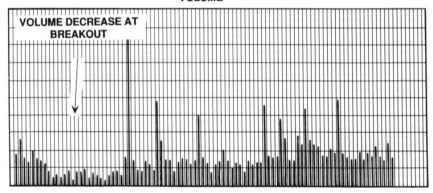

VOLUME

Figure 7.23
RECTANGLE CHANGES TO DOWNTREND

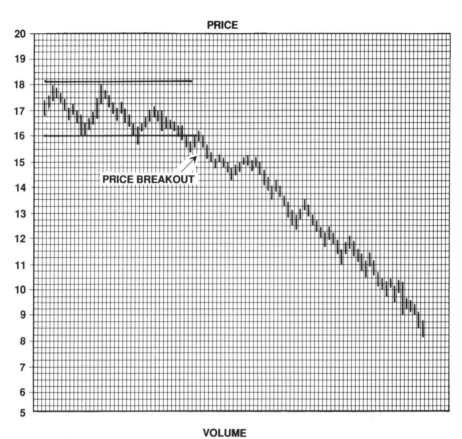

PRICE

PRICE BREAKOUT

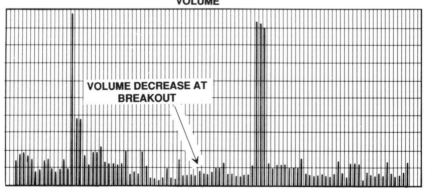

VOLUME

VOLUME DECREASE AT
BREAKOUT

Figure 7.24
SYMMETRICAL TRIANGLES

PRICE

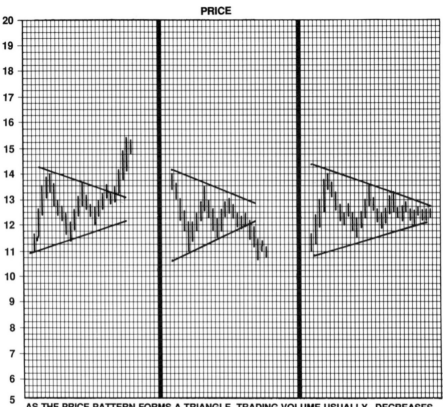

AS THE PRICE PATTERN FORMS A TRIANGLE, TRADING VOLUME USUALLY DECREASES.

VOLUME

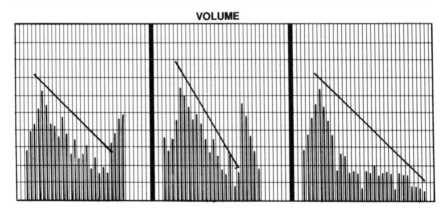

Figure 7.25
ASCENDING TRIANGLES

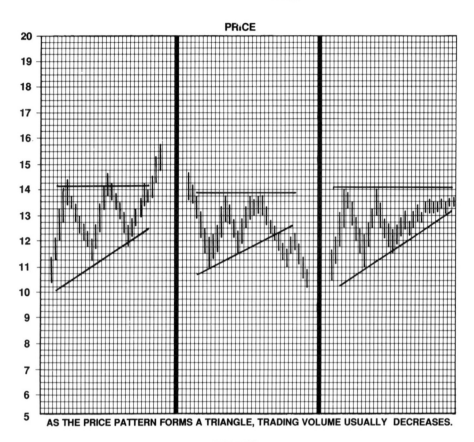

PRıCE

AS THE PRICE PATTERN FORMS A TRIANGLE, TRADING VOLUME USUALLY DECREASES.

VOLUME

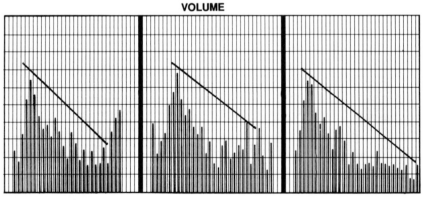

Figure 7.26
DESCENDING TRIANGLES

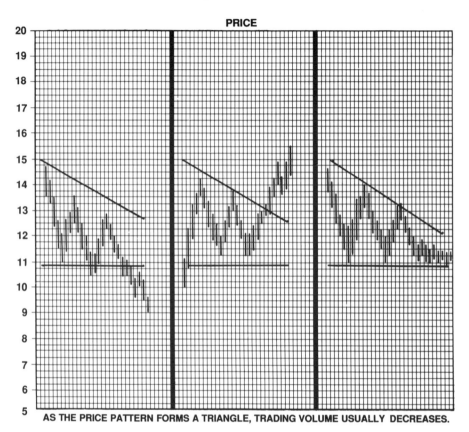

PRICE

AS THE PRICE PATTERN FORMS A TRIANGLE, TRADING VOLUME USUALLY DECREASES.

VOLUME

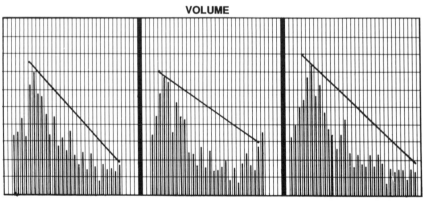

these figures for a stock of interest to you, you can compare the current increase in trading volume to the average trading volume for each stock.

A FINAL NOTE ON VOLUME

In reviewing price-and-volume charts, keep the following point in mind: no matter how many price-and-volume charts you look at, you will never see two that have the exact same pattern of price and volume of daily trading. Each chart is unique. All of the sample charts provided in this book are intended only for the purpose of illustration. They are not presented as models or as ideal cases.

Chapter Eight

MAKING INVESTMENT DECISIONS

Chapter 7 described the basic relationships between price patterns and the volume of trading. This chapter gives you the opportunity to practice making investment decisions using this knowledge. In making these decisions you will have several objectives:

- To select stocks that have a high probability for capital gains.
- To identify stocks that should be held (once bought) for further capital gains.
- To determine when stocks should be sold to protect your capital gains.

BUY OR SELL EXERCISE

Review Figures 8E.1–8E.16. Decide whether each stock should be bought or sold. Choose either alternative; indicate your decision by checking the *buy* or *sell* response. To help you make your decision, you may wish to use a ruler to draw in the appropriate trend line, neckline, or boundary lines. See Appendix A for answers.

SELL OR HOLD EXERCISE

Review the sets of paired stock price patterns in Figures 8E.17–8E.26. Assume that you own both stocks in each pair. One should be sold and the other held for additional gains. Check the appropriate response to indicate which you would hold and which you would sell. To help you make your decision, you may wish to use a ruler to draw in the appropriate trend line, neckline, or boundary lines. See Appendix A for the correct answers.

Figure 8E.1
SHOULD THIS STOCK BE BOUGHT OR SOLD?

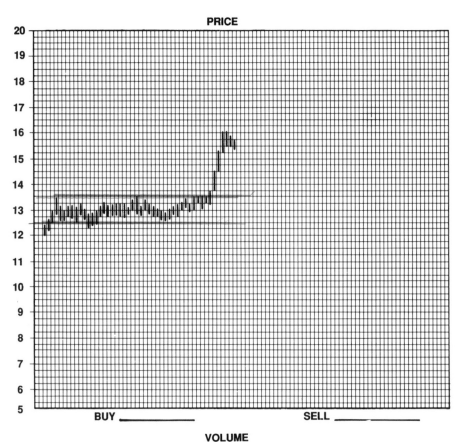

PRICE

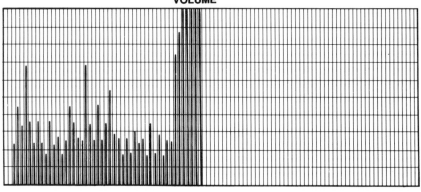

BUY _____   SELL ____ _____

VOLUME

Figure 8E.2
SHOULD THIS STOCK BE BOUGHT OR SOLD?

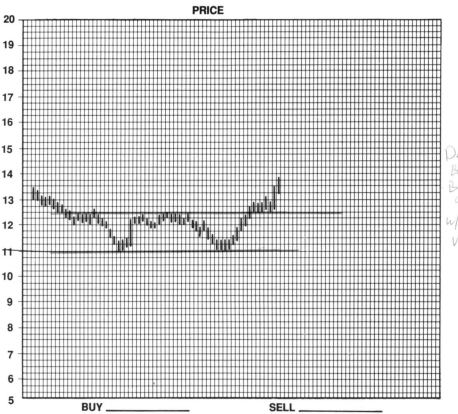

PRICE

BUY _____   SELL _____

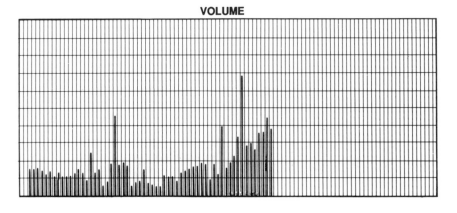

VOLUME

Figure 8E.3
SHOULD THIS STOCK BE BOUGHT OR SOLD?

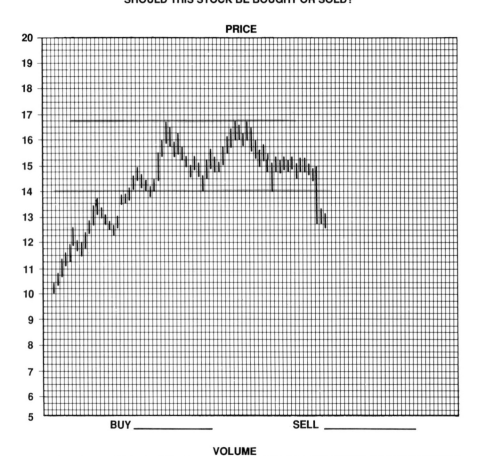

PRICE

BUY _____   SELL _____

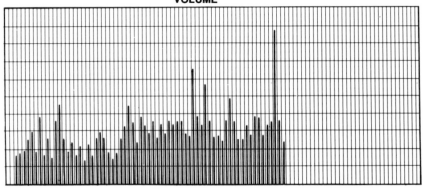

VOLUME

Figure 8E.4
SHOULD THIS STOCK BE BOUGHT OR SOLD?

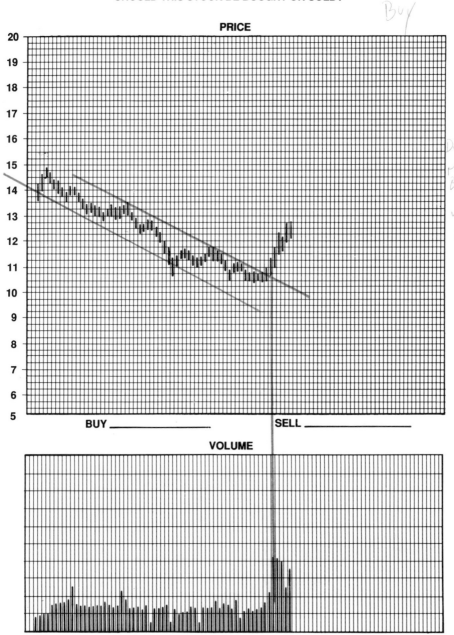

Figure 8E.5
SHOULD THIS STOCK BE BOUGHT OR SOLD?

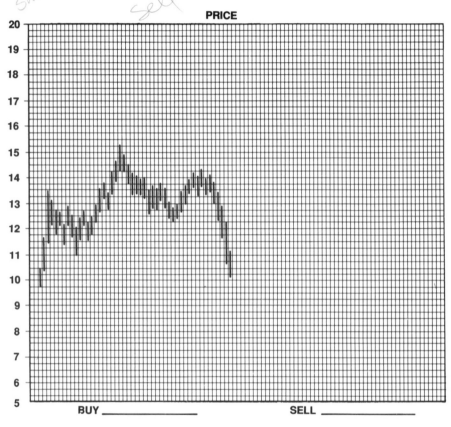

ascending head & Shoulders up/down Breakout

Sell

PRICE

BUY _____   SELL _____

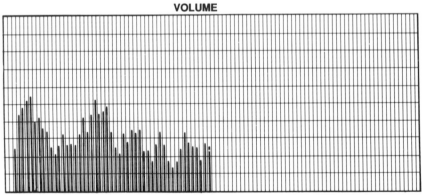

VOLUME

Figure 8E.6
SHOULD THIS STOCK BE BOUGHT OR SOLD?

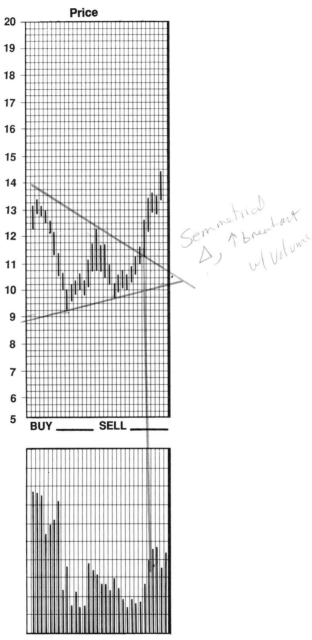

Semmetical Δ, ↑ breakort w/ Volume

Figure 8E.7
SHOULD THIS STOCK BE BOUGHT OR SOLD?

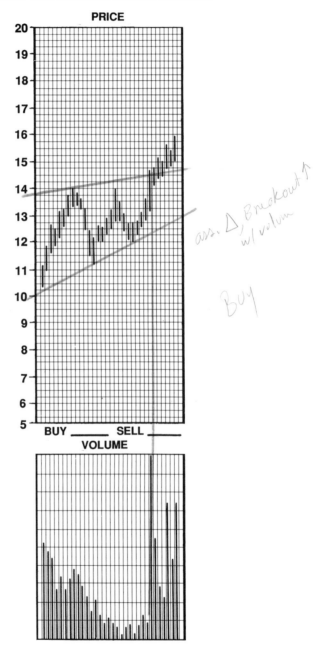

Figure 8E.8
SHOULD THIS STOCK BE BOUGHT OR SOLD?

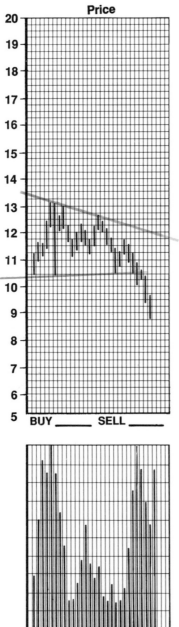

Descending △
w/ ↓ Breakout! ↑ vol

Sell

BUY _____ SELL _____

Rounded Bottom ↑swing vol/vol Buy

Figure 8E.9
SHOULD THIS STOCK BE BOUGHT OR SOLD?

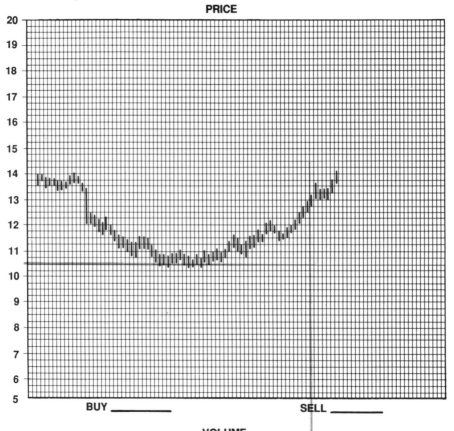

PRICE

BUY _____   SELL _____

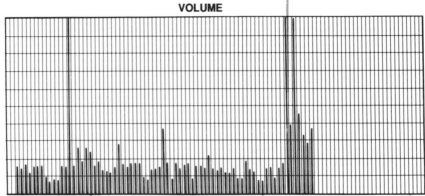

VOLUME

Figure 8E.10
SHOULD THIS STOCK BE BOUGHT OR SOLD?

Rounded top
Breakout ↓
Sell

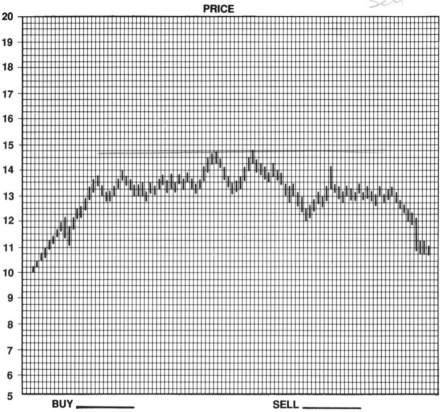

PRICE

BUY _____ SELL _____

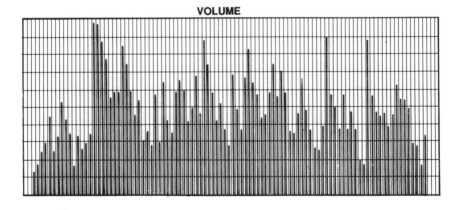

VOLUME

Figure 8E.11
SHOULD THIS STOCK BE BOUGHT OR SOLD?

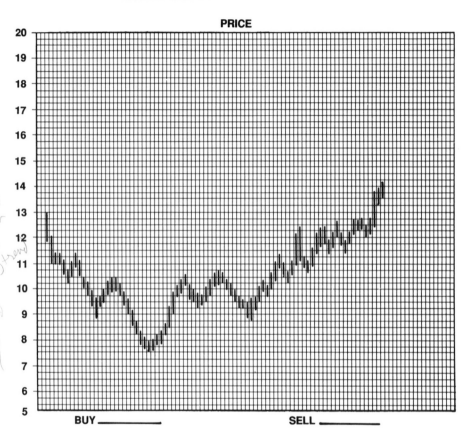

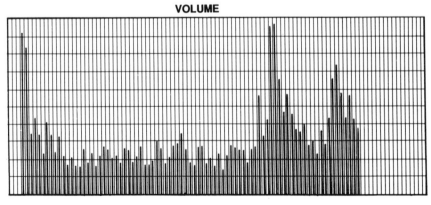

Rectangle
TRIPPLE Bottom/Top
w/ Breakout
Sell

Figure 8E.12
SHOULD THIS STOCK BE BOUGHT OR SOLD?

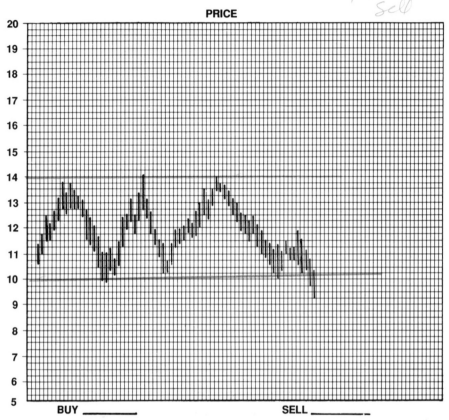

PRICE

BUY _____   SELL _____

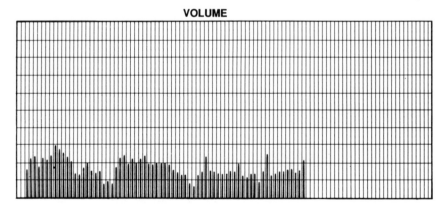

VOLUME

Rectangle Breakout ↑ w/ Vol Buy

Figure 8E.13
SHOULD THIS STOCK BE BOUGHT OR SOLD?

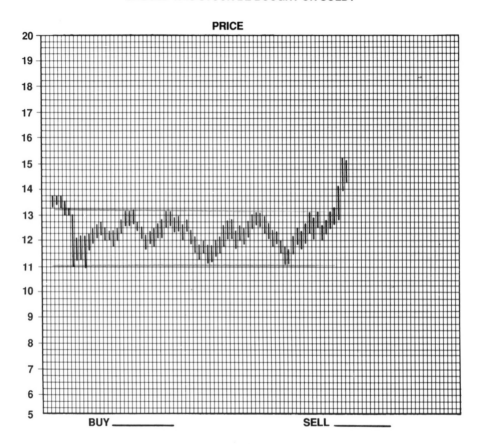

PRICE

BUY _____   SELL _____

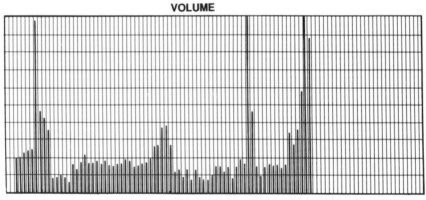

VOLUME

Figure 8E.14

A sudden Breakout
sell

SHOULD THIS STOCK BE BOUGHT OR SOLD?

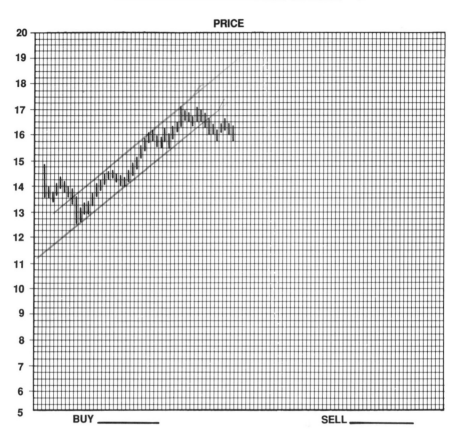

PRICE

BUY _____   SELL _____

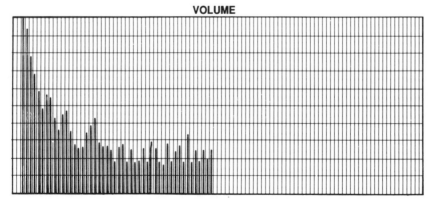

VOLUME

Rectangle Breakout
w/ Volume Buy

Figure 8E.15
SHOULD THIS STOCK BE BOUGHT OR SOLD?

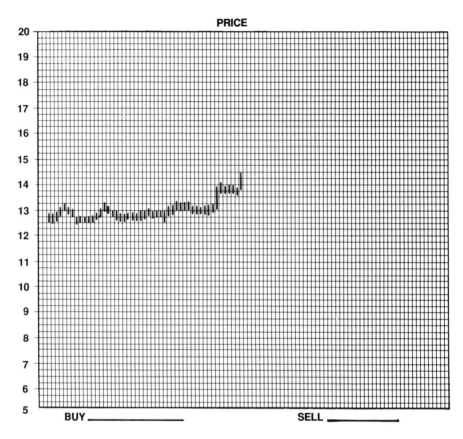

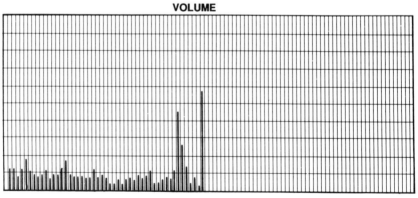

TRIPLE TOP

breakout ↓

Figure 8E.16
SHOULD THIS STOCK BE BOUGHT OR SOLD?

PRICE

BUY _____   SELL _____

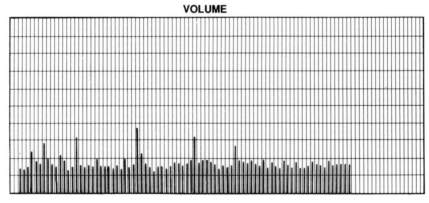

VOLUME

Figure 8E.17
WHICH STOCK SHOULD BE SOLD AND WHICH SHOULD BE HELD?

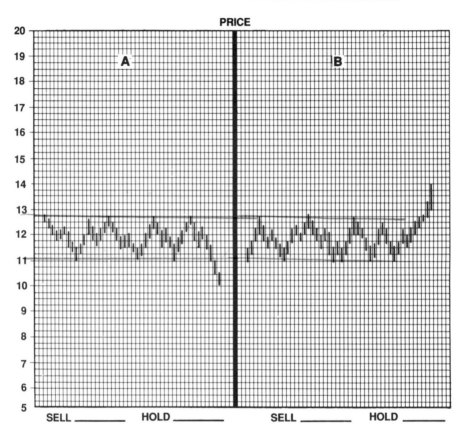

PRICE

SELL _____ **HOLD** _____   **SELL** _____ **HOLD** _____

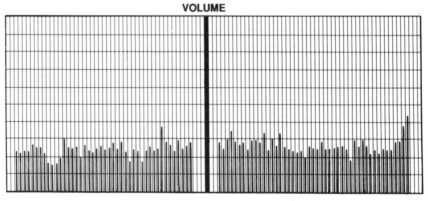

VOLUME

Figure 8E.18
WHICH STOCK SHOULD BE SOLD AND WHICH SHOULD BE HELD?

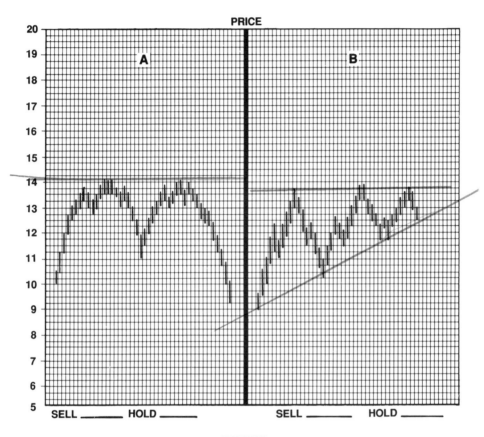

PRICE

SELL _____ HOLD _____   SELL _____ HOLD _____

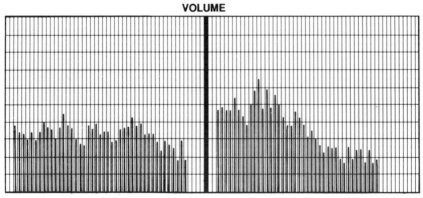

VOLUME

Figure 8E.19
WHICH STOCK SHOULD BE SOLD AND WHICH SHOULD BE HELD?

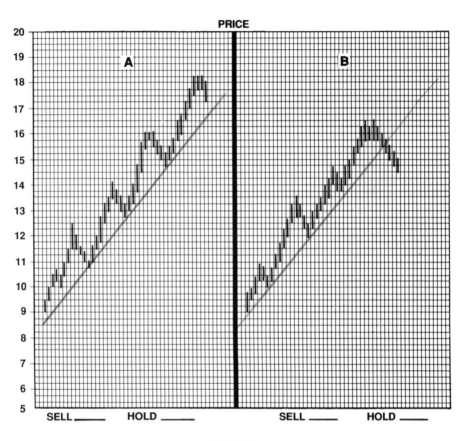

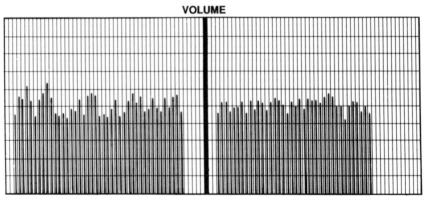

Figure 8E.20
WHICH STOCK SHOULD BE SOLD AND WHICH SHOULD BE HELD?

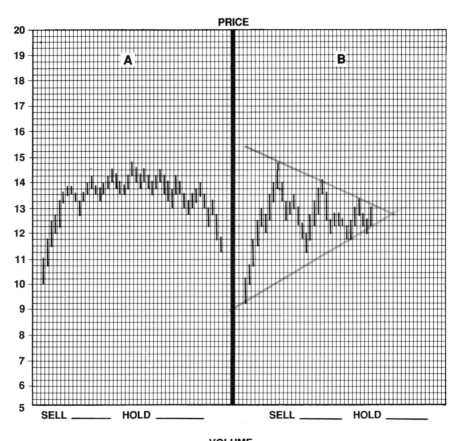

PRICE

A   B

SELL _____ HOLD _____   SELL _____ HOLD _____

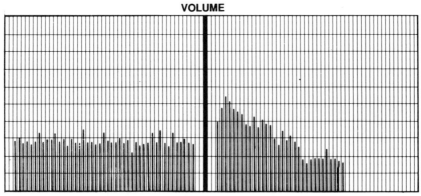

VOLUME

Figure 8E.21
WHICH STOCK SHOULD BE SOLD AND WHICH SHOULD BE HELD?

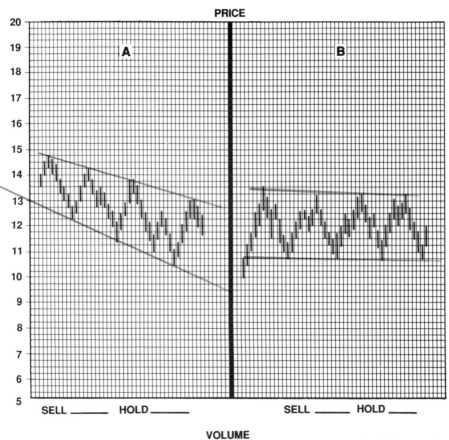

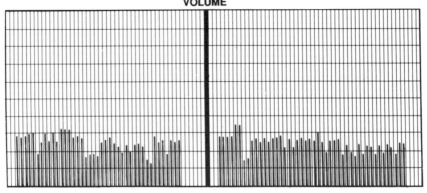

Figure 8E.22
WHICH STOCK SHOULD BE SOLD AND WHICH SHOULD BE HELD?

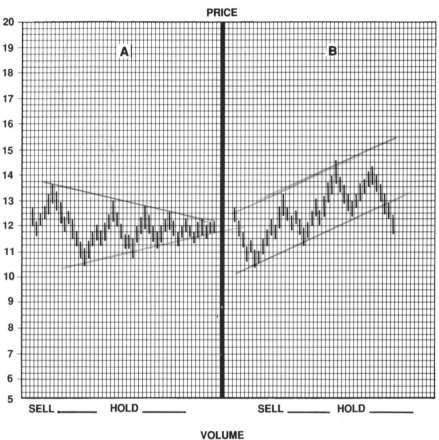

PRICE

A   B

SELL _____ HOLD _____   SELL _____ HOLD _____

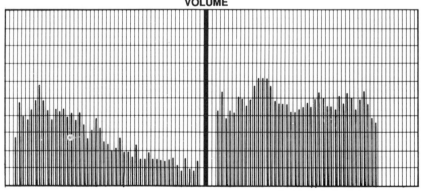

VOLUME

Figure 8E.23
WHICH STOCK SHOULD BE SOLD AND WHICH SHOULD BE HELD?

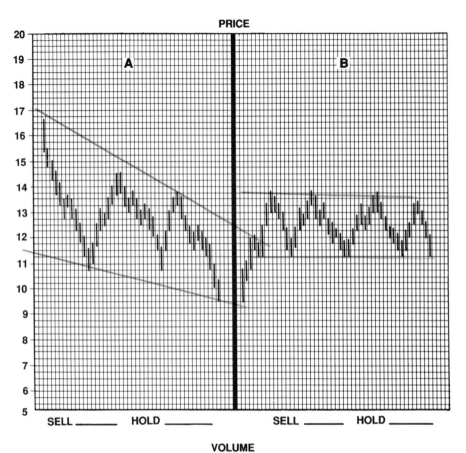

PRICE

A   B

SELL _____   HOLD _____   SELL _____   HOLD _____

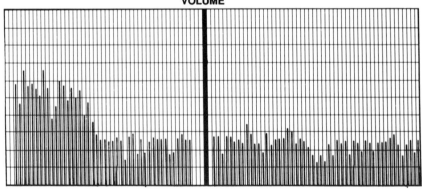

VOLUME

Figure 8E.24
WHICH STOCK SHOULD BE SOLD AND WHICH SHOULD BE HELD?

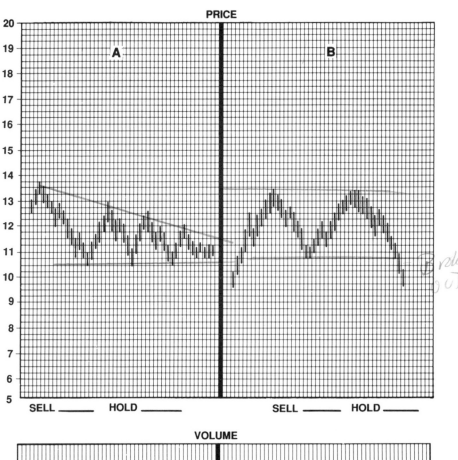

PRICE

A   B

SELL _____   HOLD _____   SELL _____   HOLD _____

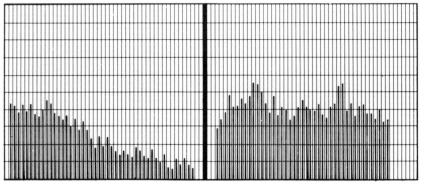

VOLUME

head & shoulder

Figure 8E.25
WHICH STOCK SHOULD BE SOLD AND WHICH SHOULD BE HELD?

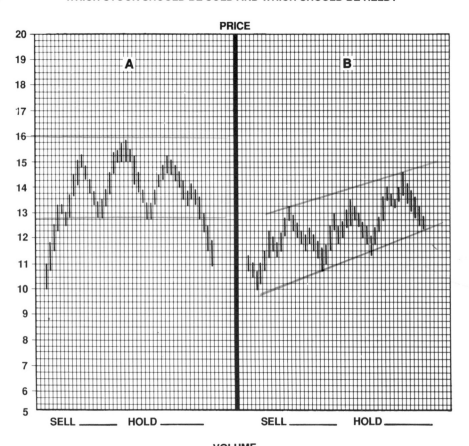

SELL _____ HOLD _____   SELL _____ HOLD _____

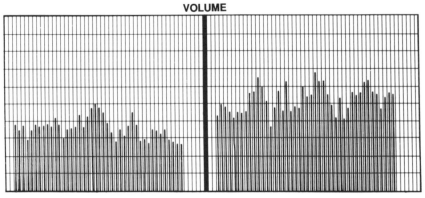

Figure 8E.26
WHICH STOCK SHOULD BE SOLD AND WHICH SHOULD BE HELD?

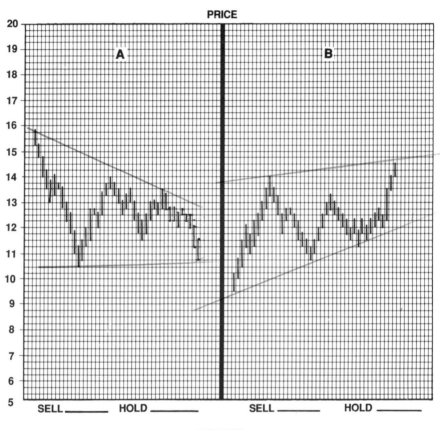

PRICE

A   B

SELL _____ HOLD _____   SELL _____ HOLD _____

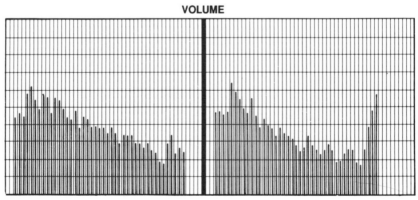

VOLUME

BUY SELECTION EXERCISE

The stock price patterns in Figures 8E.27–8E.37 are presented in pairs. Study each pair and decide which stock should be bought. Select the stock you believe has the higher probability for a rise in price. To help you make your decision, you may wish to use a ruler to draw in the appropriate trend line, neckline, or boundary lines. Indicate your selection by checking the *buy* response under your choice. See Appendix A for the correct answers.

Price Pattern Identification

Examine the price patterns in Figures 8E.38–8E.56. Identify each pattern and write its name in the space provided below the price section of the chart. Then decide which courses of action would be best: buy, sell, or wait for additional data on price and volume of trading. When you have chosen one of these three alternatives, indicate your decision by checking the *buy*, *sell*, or *wait* response. See Appendix A for the correct answers.

ON YOUR OWN

The practical aspects of starting to use charts to make investment decisions are fairly straightforward. Prepared charts are available from several publishers, or you can prepare the charts yourself. You can decide which approach best suits your inclinations and meets your needs. Some of the publishers that prepare and sell charts are listed here. I recommend you use charts that are posted daily as these are the most revealing.

Stock Chart Publishers

Daily Graphs P.0. Box 66919 Los Angeles, CA 90099	Charts posted daily and published weekly are available.
Trendline, Inc. 25 Broadway New York, NY 10004	Charts posted daily and published weekly are available.
Mansfield Stock Charts 2973 Kennedy Blvd. Jersey City, NJ 07306	Charts posted weekly and published weekly are available.
Securities Research Corp. 101 Prescott St. Wellesley Hills, MA 02181	Charts posted weekly and published weekly are available.

Figure 8E.27
WHICH STOCK SHOULD BE BOUGHT?

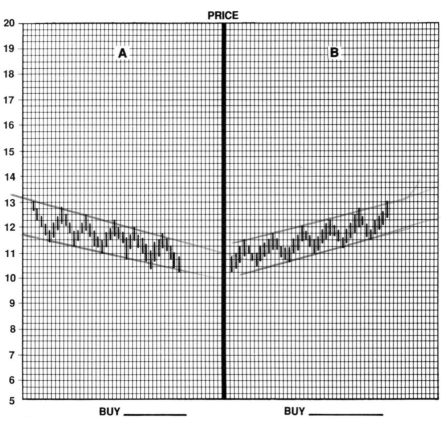

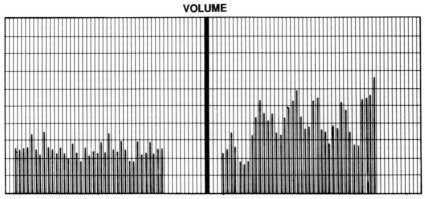

Figure 8E.28
WHICH STOCK SHOULD BE BOUGHT?

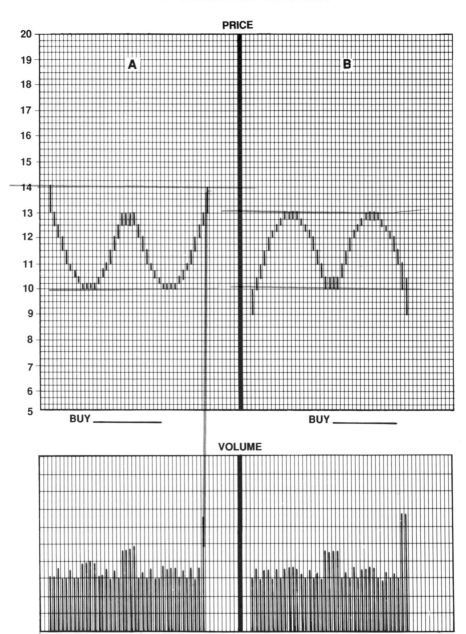

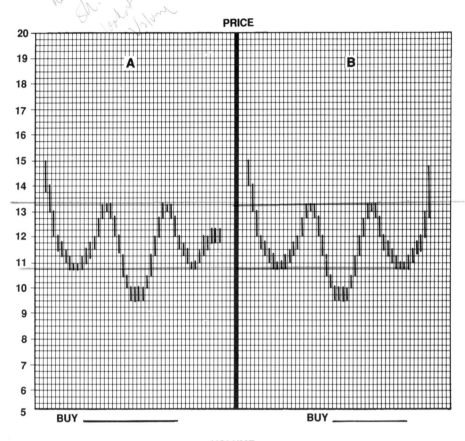

Figure 8E.29
WHICH STOCK SHOULD BE BOUGHT?

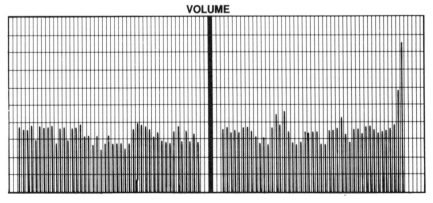

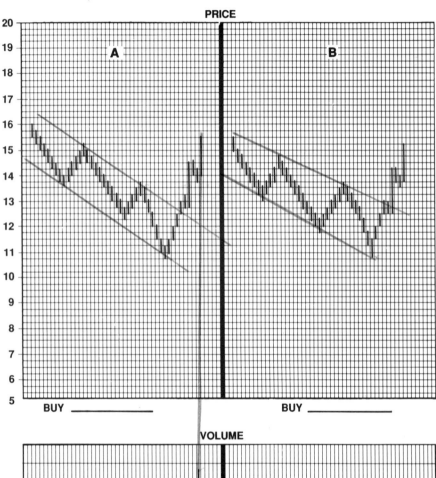

Figure 8E.30
WHICH STOCK SHOULD BE BOUGHT?

PRICE

A

B

BUY _____   BUY _____

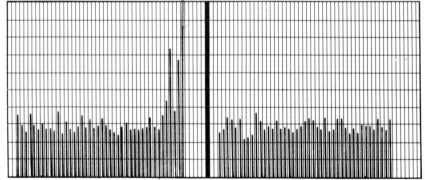

VOLUME

Figure 8E.31
WHICH STOCK SHOULD BE BOUGHT?

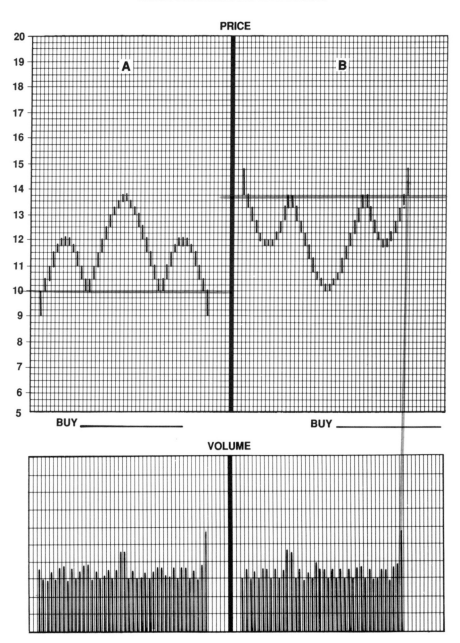

Figure 8E.32

WHICH STOCK SHOULD BE BOUGHT?

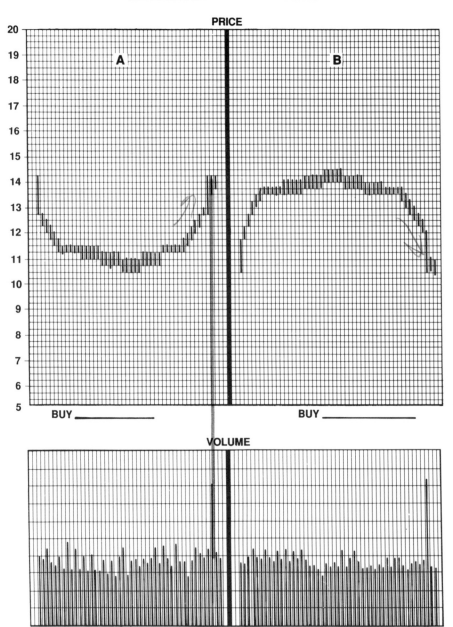

Figure 8E.33
WHICH STOCK SHOULD BE BOUGHT?

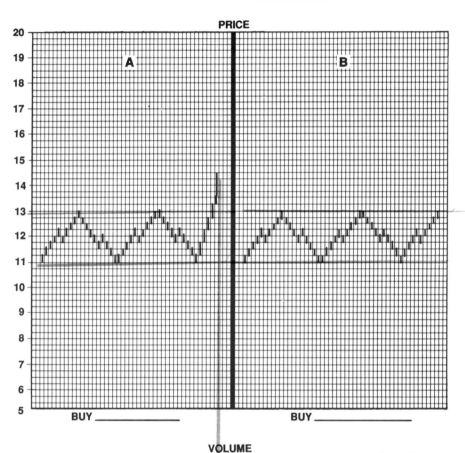

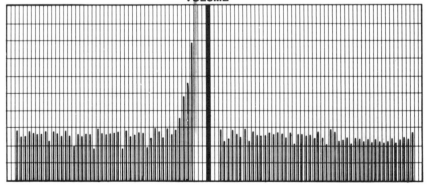

Figure 8E.34
WHICH STOCK SHOULD BE BOUGHT?

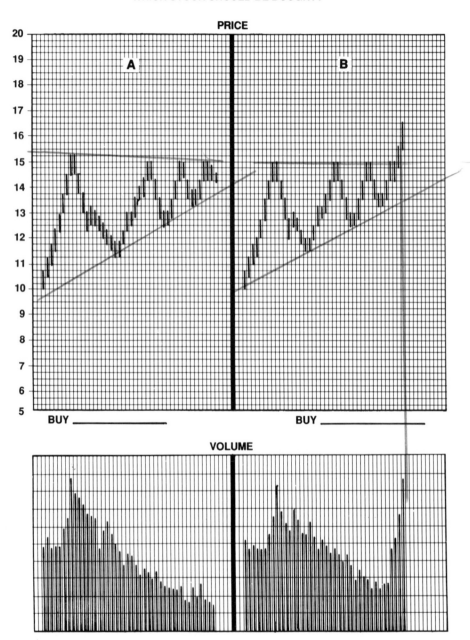

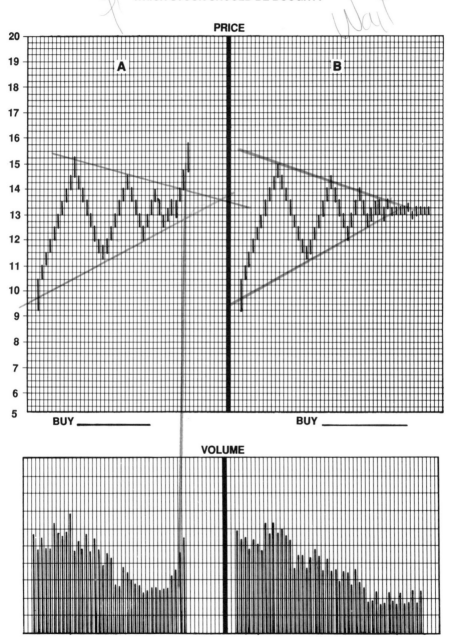

Figure 8E.35
WHICH STOCK SHOULD BE BOUGHT?

Figure 8E.36
WHICH STOCK SHOULD BE BOUGHT?

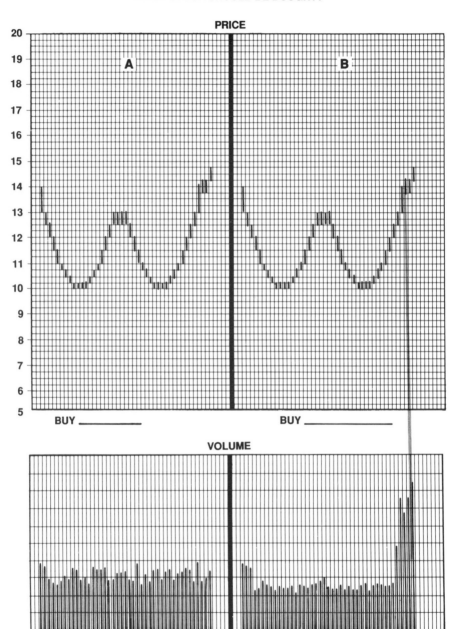

Figure 8E.37
WHICH STOCK SHOULD BE BOUGHT?

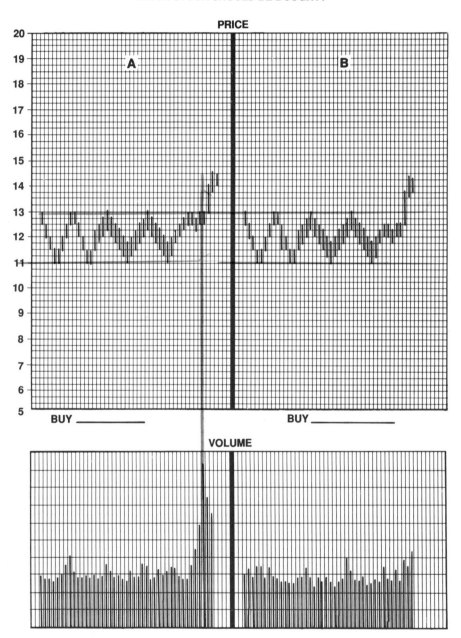

Figure 8E.38

WHAT IS THE NAME OF THIS PATTERN?
SHOULD YOU BUY, SELL, OR WAIT FOR MORE DATA?

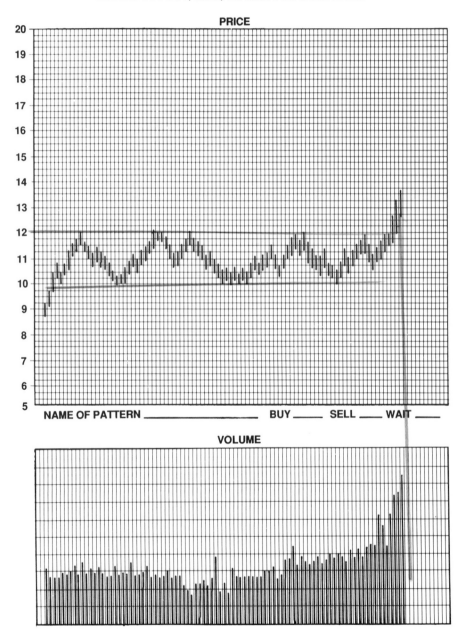

NAME OF PATTERN _____ BUY _____ SELL _____ WAIT _____

Figure 8E.39

**WHAT IS THE NAME OF THIS PATTERN?
SHOULD YOU BUY, SELL, OR WAIT FOR MORE DATA?**

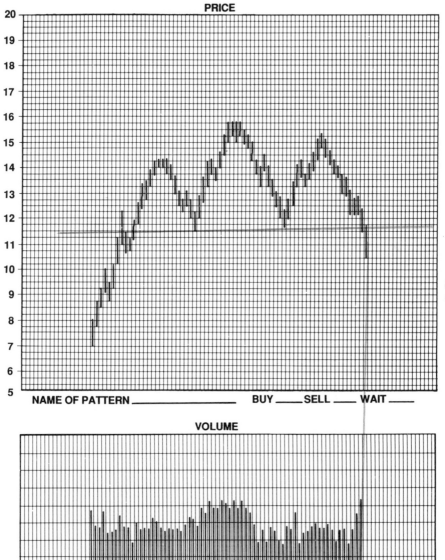

NAME OF PATTERN _____ BUY ____ SELL ____ WAIT ____

uptrend w ex pandry)
volume
BUY

Figure 8E.40

WHAT IS THE NAME OF THIS PATTERN?
SHOULD YOU BUY, SELL, OR WAIT FOR MORE DATA?

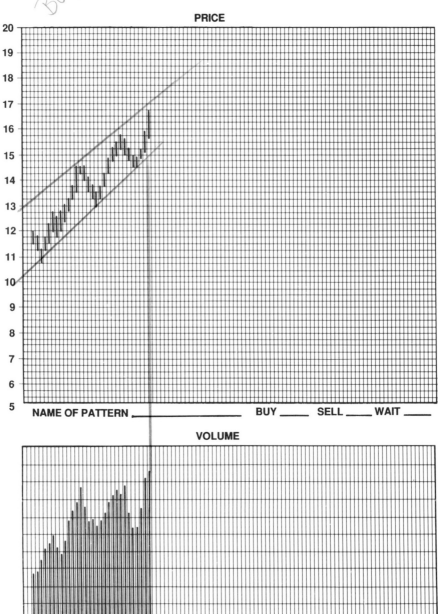

NAME OF PATTERN _____   BUY ____ SELL ____ WAIT ____

Figure 8E.41
WHAT IS THE NAME OF THIS PATTERN?
SHOULD YOU BUY, SELL, OR WAIT FOR MORE DATA?

PRICE

NAME OF PATTERN _____ BUY ____ SELL ____ WAIT ____

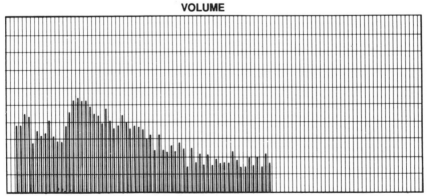

VOLUME

Figure 8E.42

WHAT IS THE NAME OF THIS PATTERN?
SHOULD YOU BUY, SELL, OR WAIT FOR MORE DATA?

TRIPLE Bottom Breen out w/ Volum Buy

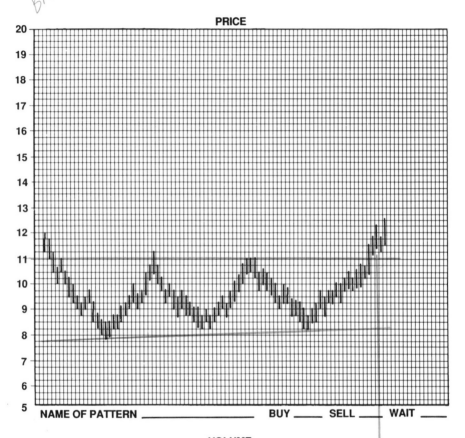

PRICE

NAME OF PATTERN _____ BUY _____ SELL _____ WAIT _____

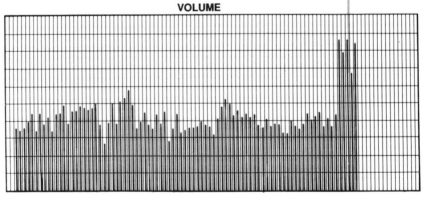

VOLUME

Figure 8E.43

WHAT IS THE NAME OF THIS PATTERN?
SHOULD YOU BUY, SELL, OR WAIT FOR MORE DATA?

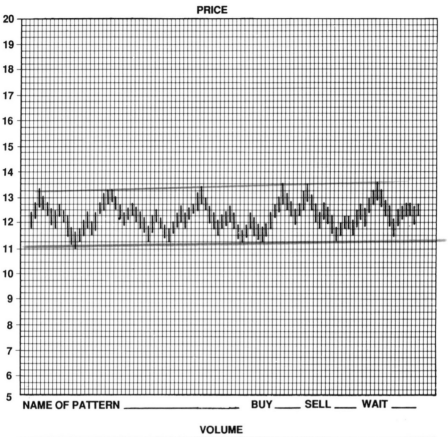

PRICE

NAME OF PATTERN _____ BUY ____ SELL ____ WAIT ____

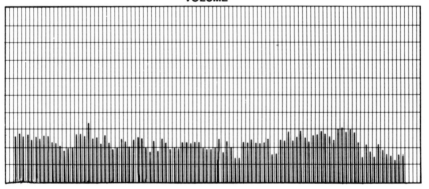

VOLUME

Figure 8E.44

WHAT IS THE NAME OF THIS PATTERN?
SHOULD YOU BUY, SELL, OR WAIT FOR MORE DATA?

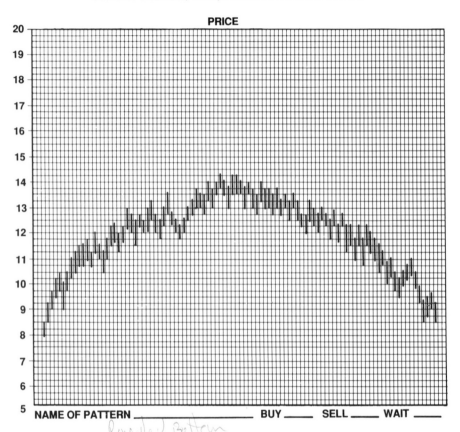

PRICE

NAME OF PATTERN _____ BUY _____ SELL _____ WAIT _____

Rounded Bottom

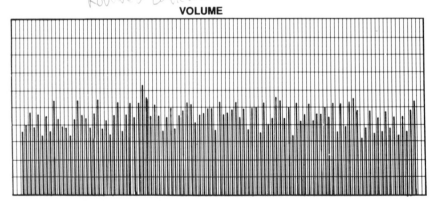

VOLUME

Figure 8E.45
WHAT IS THE NAME OF THIS PATTERN?
SHOULD YOU BUY, SELL, OR WAIT FOR MORE DATA?

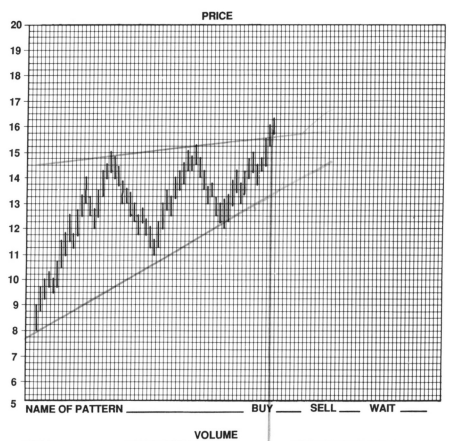

PRICE

NAME OF PATTERN _____ BUY _____ SELL _____ WAIT _____

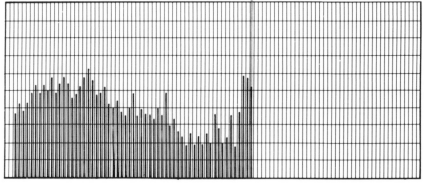

VOLUME

Figure 8E.46

WHAT IS THE NAME OF THIS PATTERN?
SHOULD YOU BUY, SELL, OR WAIT FOR MORE DATA?

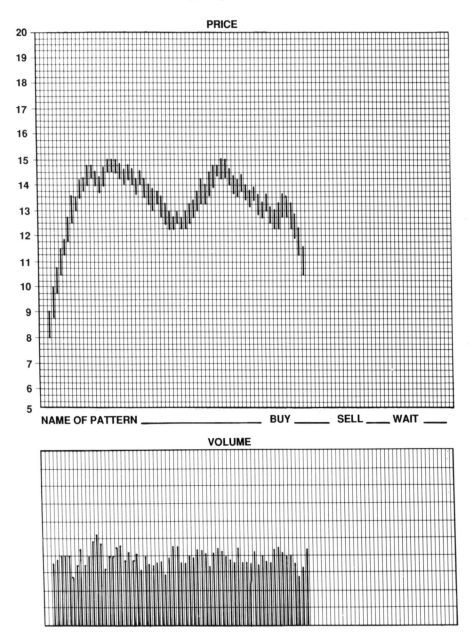

NAME OF PATTERN _____ BUY _____ SELL ____ WAIT ____

Figure 8E.47

WHAT IS THE NAME OF THIS PATTERN?
SHOULD YOU BUY, SELL, OR WAIT FOR MORE DATA?

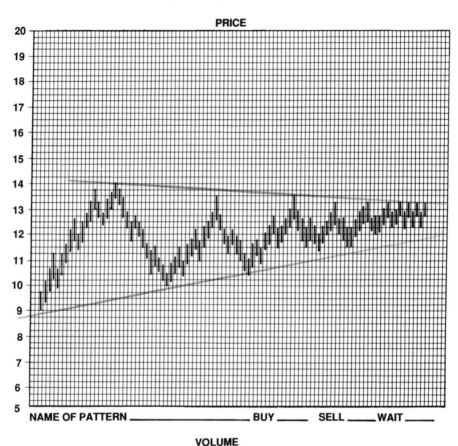

PRICE

NAME OF PATTERN _____ BUY _____ SELL _____ WAIT _____

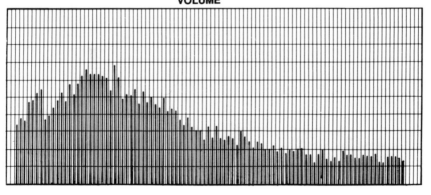

VOLUME

Figure 8E.48
WHAT IS THE NAME OF THIS PATTERN?
SHOULD YOU BUY, SELL, OR WAIT FOR MORE DATA?

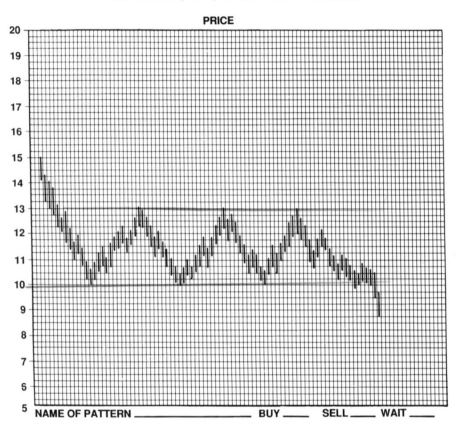

NAME OF PATTERN _____ BUY ___ SELL ___ WAIT ___

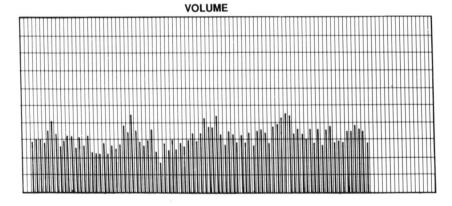

Figure 8E.49

WHAT IS THE NAME OF THIS PATTERN?
SHOULD YOU BUY, SELL, OR WAIT FOR MORE DATA?

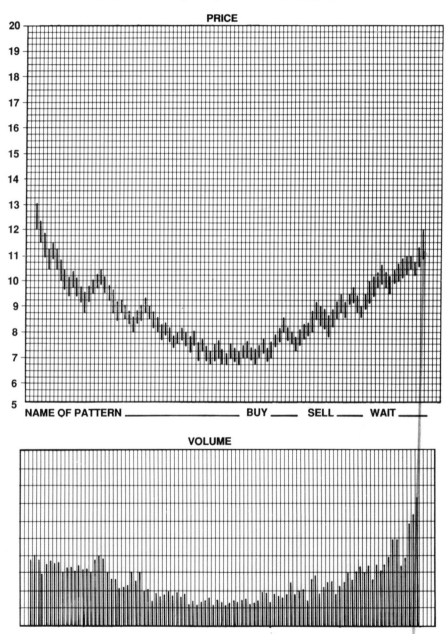

NAME OF PATTERN _____ BUY _____ SELL _____ WAIT _____

Figure 8E.50

WHAT IS THE NAME OF THIS PATTERN?
SHOULD YOU BUY, SELL, OR WAIT FOR MORE DATA?

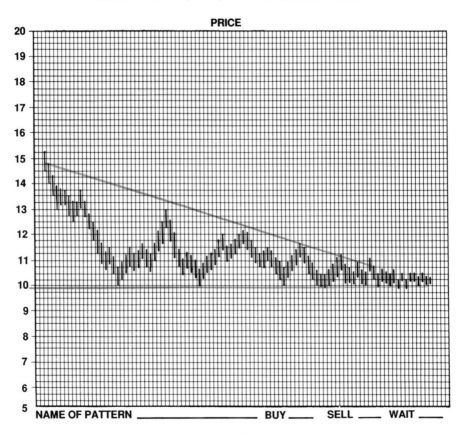

PRICE

NAME OF PATTERN _____ BUY ____ SELL ____ WAIT ____

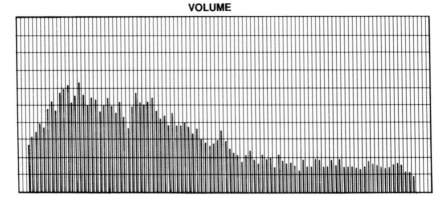

VOLUME

Figure 8E.51

WHAT IS THE NAME OF THIS PATTERN?
SHOULD YOU BUY, SELL, OR WAIT FOR MORE DATA?

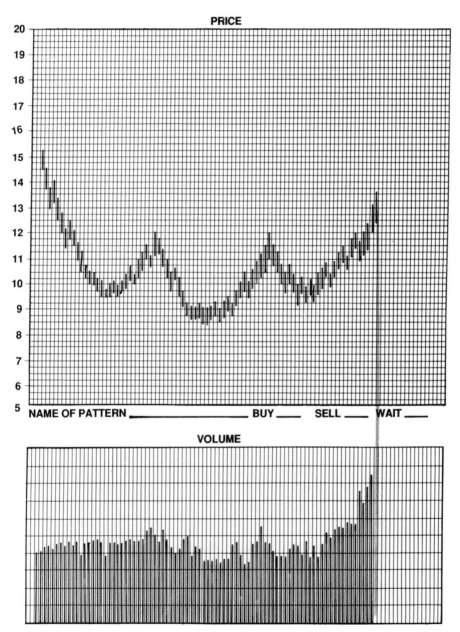

NAME OF PATTERN _____ BUY ____ SELL ____ WAIT ____

Figure 8E.52

WHAT IS THE NAME OF THIS PATTERN?
SHOULD YOU BUY, SELL, OR WAIT FOR MORE DATA?

PRICE

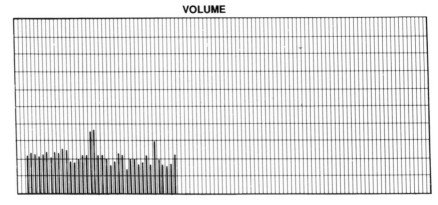

NAME OF PATTERN _____ BUY _____ SELL _____ WAIT _____

VOLUME

Figure 8E.53

WHAT IS THE NAME OF THIS PATTERN?
SHOULD YOU BUY, SELL, OR WAIT FOR MORE DATA?

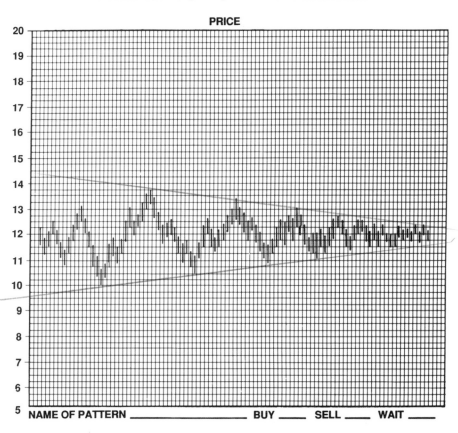

PRICE

NAME OF PATTERN _____ BUY _____ SELL _____ WAIT _____

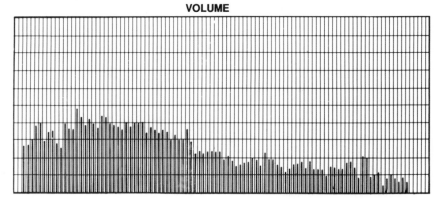

VOLUME

Figure 8E.54

WHAT IS THE NAME OF THIS PATTERN?
SHOULD YOU BUY, SELL, OR WAIT FOR MORE DATA?

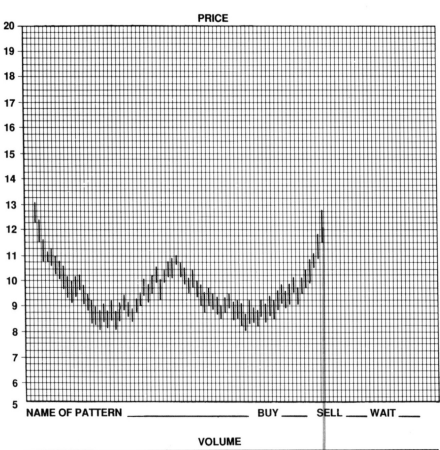

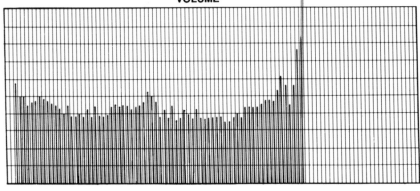

NAME OF PATTERN _____ BUY ____ SELL ____ WAIT ____

Figure 8E.55
WHAT IS THE NAME OF THIS PATTERN?
SHOULD YOU BUY, SELL, OR WAIT FOR MORE DATA?

PRICE

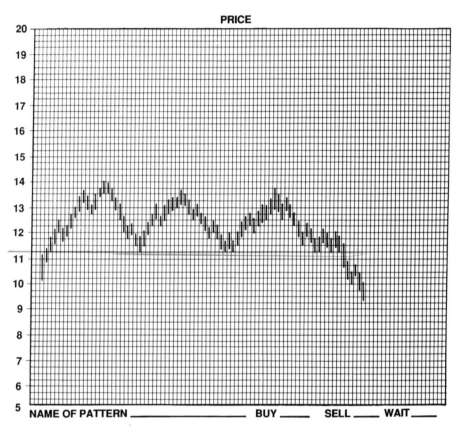

NAME OF PATTERN _____ BUY _____ SELL _____ WAIT_____

VOLUME

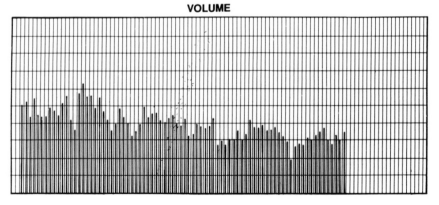

Figure 8E.56

WHAT IS THE NAME OF THIS PATTERN?
SHOULD YOU BUY, SELL, OR WAIT FOR MORE DATA?

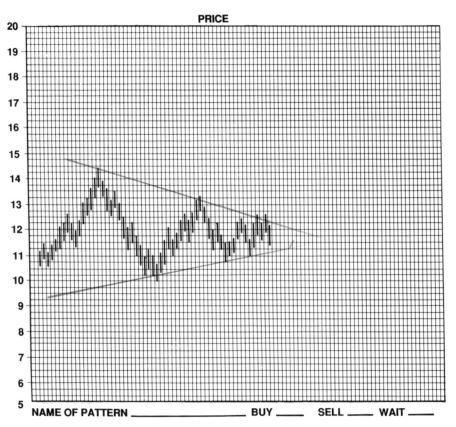

NAME OF PATTERN _____ BUY _____ SELL _____ WAIT _____

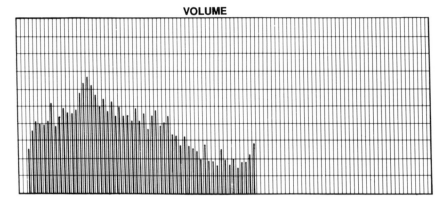

Before selecting a chart publisher, visit the main branch of your public library. Your library may subscribe to several charting services. If so, you will have an opportunity to decide which one best suits your needs.

If you are willing to spend a few minutes a day, you can make your own charts. The price and volume information you would post is published daily in the financial section of many newspapers. I recommend that you make your own charts so that you will have information which is current on a daily basis rather than weekly. If you decide to make your own charts, you can buy chart paper from your local engineering supply outlet. The Keuffel and Esser Company is a national distributor of a wide variety of chart paper. You can order chart paper from John Magee, Inc., 103 State St., Boston, MA 02109. The chart paper distributed by this company is suitable for charting stocks; it has separate sections for showing prices and daily trading volume as they relate to each other.

Pages 160–162 provide several blank charts for you to use until you decide which type of published chart or chart paper you want to use. No price or volume figures are printed on these charts. You can enter those figures that apply to the stocks you wish to chart. If you use these charts, you may want to remove them from the book and attach them side by side to allow for a longer period of time to be displayed.

PRICE

VOLUME

PRICE

VOLUME

PRICE

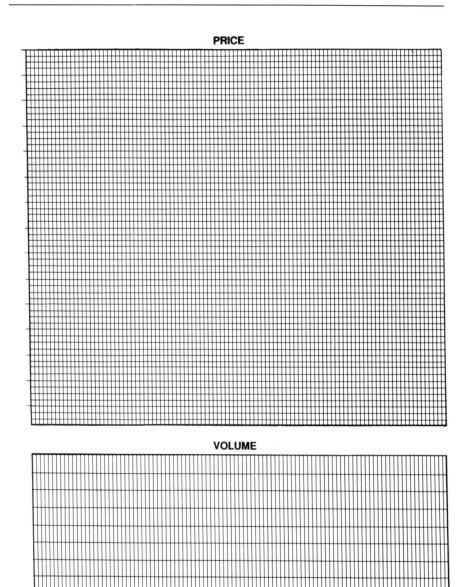

VOLUME

Chapter Nine

MOVING AVERAGES

There are no guarantees in the stock market. The penetration of a boundary line, trend line, support, or resistance level does not always produce the expected result. Price and volume patterns are not always reliable. Here are some examples. A breakout above a resistance level on high volume may be followed by a quick drop back to the starting point. This type of sharp up and down price movement is referred to as a "spike." (Subsequent price movement can be up, down, or sideways.) Any rise above a resistance level can be followed by an extended downtrend. This type of deceptive breakout is referred to as a "bull trap." Similarly, a plunge below a support level can be followed by an extended uptrend. This deceptive downside penetration is referred to as a "bear trap." The breakout from some ascending triangles is to the downside and a breakout from some descending triangles is to the upside. These and other contrary occurrences give rise to the conclusion that price and volume patterns are not completely reliable.

The purpose of this chapter and the next is to improve the reliability of your interpretations through the use of additional techniques and data. You will learn to use moving averages, accumulation, and distribution data in combination with price patterns, trend lines, and volume to decide when to buy, how long to hold, and when to sell.

DEFINITION OF A MOVING AVERAGE

A moving average is a consecutive series of stock price averages. For example, a 10-day moving average is derived by summing the closing prices of the most recent 10 days and dividing that total by 10 to arrive at the average price. A dot is placed on the chart at the appropriate point to represent this price. The following day the most recent closing price is added to the total and the oldest is removed from the total. The average price of this latest 10-day period is then calculated and another dot is put on the chart next to the previous point. On each successive day, the average price for the most recent set of 10 days of closing prices is plotted on the chart, and this series of dots becomes the moving average.

Because a moving average is calculated from previous prices, it lags behind current prices. Since it is constructed from many prices, it smooths out the daily price fluctuations to identify the price trend. (See Figure 9.1.)

Relationship between Moving Average and Trend Line

As shown in Chapters 2 through 8, price trends and trading volume can be analyzed without reference to moving averages. There are several conditions under which you may want to do this. First, some published charts do not show moving averages. Second, some commercially prepared charts may not show an average that is appropriate for your objectives. For example, if your objective is long-term capital gain, a short or intermediate moving average will not lend itself to that purpose. Similarly, if there are occasions when you want to focus on a short- or intermediate-term gain, a long-term moving average will not be helpful.

Third, if you prepare your own charts, you may not want to do the extra work of calculating moving averages. In any of those situations, you may decide to analyze a chart without referring to a moving average.

In general, though, a moving average used in conjunction with a trend line, can broaden and improve your stock chart interpretations as follows:

- An uptrend line and a rising moving average provide double confirmation that an uptrend is in progress.

- An uptrend can be regarded as still valid even after the penetration of the uptrend line if the moving average has not also been penetrated to the downside.

- An uptrend can be regarded as still valid after the downside penetration of a moving average if the uptrend line has not also been penetrated.

- When both the uptrend line and the moving average have been penetrated to the downside, you have confirmation that the uptrend has ended.

Figures 9.1 through 9.3 illustrate these relationships between trend lines and moving averages.

Because of their different characteristics, short, intermediate, and long moving averages are best used in specific applications. Some uses for each length are described below.

LONG MOVING AVERAGES

Long-term uptrends can be found in the stock prices of companies in a growth industry. Along with the uptrend line, the long moving average helps you identify the rising bottoms which define the long-term price uptrend. (See Figure 9.4.)

Figure 9.1
MOVING AVERAGE SMOOTHS FLUCTUATIONS AND LAGS CURRENT PRICE

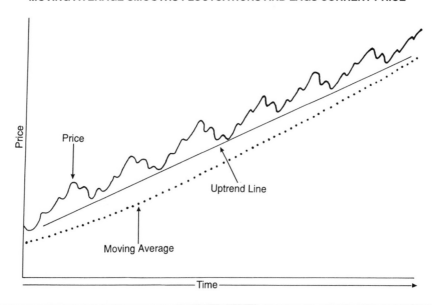

Figure 9.2
PENETRATION OF TRENDLINE NOT CONFIRMED

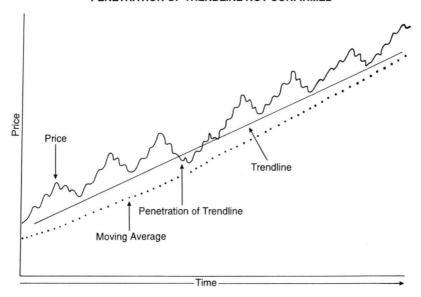

Figure 9.3

PENETRATION OF MOVING AVERAGE CONFIRMS PRICE DIRECTION CHANGE

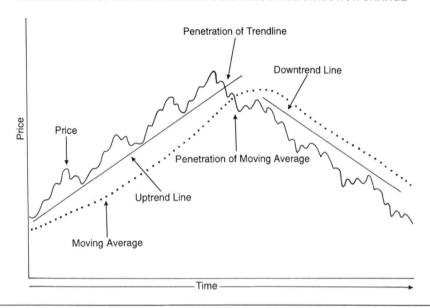

Figure 9.4

TRENDLINE AND MOVING AVERAGE CONFIRM GROWTH COMPANY UPTREND

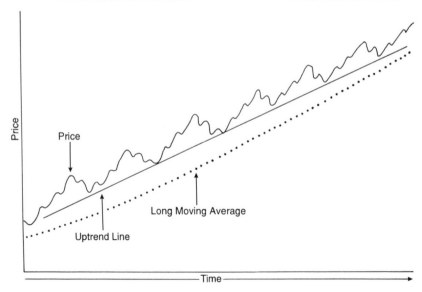

Long averages are also helpful for tracking the price fluctuations of cyclical stocks. During an upturn in the economy, cyclical companies increase their profits rapidly, and the prices of their stocks usually develop strong uptrends. An average based on a time span of 150 days or longer is likely to follow this uptrend at a sufficient distance to avoid premature penetration. When the stock price turns down, the moving average will continue rising for awhile because of its upward momentum. As the stock price falls, it penetrates the moving average to the downside—giving a sell signal. The moving average then starts to decline and follows the stock price down, lagging behind and above it. After the stock price reaches its lowest level, it start rising again and eventually penetrates the average to the upside, beginning the cycle again and giving a buy signal. (See Figure 9.5.)

Note, however, that this is an idealized representation from which there will be variations based on factors such as economic conditions and their relative impact on different industries and companies. Some industries which are affected by the business cycle in this manner are auto manufacturers, steel companies, paper and cardboard companies, aluminum and copper mining, oil companies, building materials suppliers, manufacturers and retailers of durable goods, the airlines, and companies involved in ground transportation.

INTERMEDIATE MOVING AVERAGES

Intermediate averages (51 to 149 days in length) can be used to trade intermediate-term price trends within a long-term uptrend. There are a few stocks whose intermediate price trends are smooth enough to accommodate such trading. In these cases, an intermediate average follows these price trends at a distance which allows a profitable series of buy and sell transactions such as are shown in Figure 9.6. The figure as drawn reflects the best case. Often actual price trends are not that smooth and may criss-cross the moving average more frequently, giving many buy and sell signals. The net result could be a series of transactions profitable only to the broker. For this reason, success at intermediate-term trend trading is difficult to achieve. It's best not to focus on this time frame until you have demonstrated your ability to make profitable long-term transactions.

SHORT MOVING AVERAGES

Short averages of 50 days or less are the most difficult to interpret. Because of the small amount of data used to construct them, they are more subject to distortion from rumors and other nonsignificant events which may have a strong but temporary effect on prices. There is, however, one situation in which a short-term average can have a large advantage over an intermediate or long-term one. There may come a time when you are lucky enough to hold

Figure 9.5
RELATIONSHIP BETWEEN PRICE OF CYCLICAL STOCK AND MOVING AVERAGE

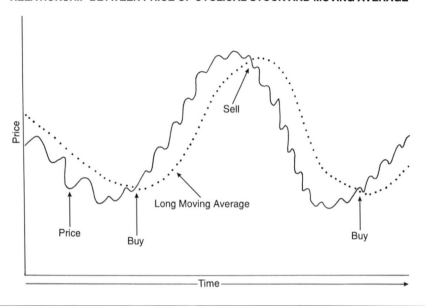

Figure 9.6
USING AN INTERMEDIATE MOVING AVERAGE TO TRADE INTERMEDIATE TRENDS

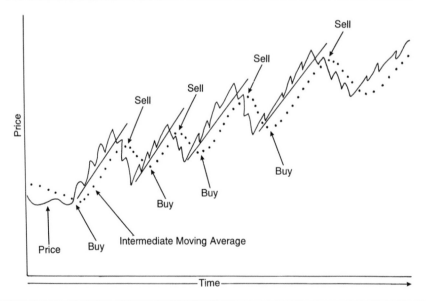

a stock in a parabolic price curve. This unique type of curve develops when a price rise accelerates until it is going almost straight up. This can be a delightful experience, but it presents a tough decision. Common sense indicates the price cannot go straight up forever. However, you don't want to sell too soon, because the price is rising so fast. In this situation, how can you determine the time to sell?

A skyrocketing price signifies that excessive speculation is in progress. When speculators see a stock moving up fast, they are eager to be in on the action. Their enthusiasm pushes the price up faster and faster, until all who want to buy have bought, and there's no one left to pay the excessively high price. When that situation develops, the price often drops as fast as it rose.

A short moving average can help you time your sale to reduce the chance of staying in too long or selling out too soon. See Figure 9.7, which illustrates the general relationship among the current price and various length moving averages. Note that the short one allows the smallest gap.

If the price of your stock traces a parabolic curve, construct an average price of 10 or 20 days, and plot it each day on the chart for that stock. (Use 10 days if you would be satisfied to take the profit you already have. Use 20 days if you have hopes for more.) Each morning place a stop sell order, "Good for the day" at the latest short average price. If the current price drops to the latest short average price, your stock will be sold automatically "at the market." This tactic can insure a sale before much or all of your profit disappears. (See Figure 9.8.)

MOVING AVERAGES IN COMMERCIAL CHART SERVICES

There are several companies which publish charted information on stocks. The charts show price fluctuations, volume of trading, and a moving average. (Some charts show two averages and many other items of interest.) Your public library may subscribe to one or more of these services. Here is information on these companies, their charts and the averages they show.

Company Name and Address	Chart Series	Length of Moving Averages
Trendline Div. of Standard & Poor's	Daily Action	50 and 150 days
25 Broadway New York, NY 10004	Current Market Perspectives	150 days
William O'Neill P.O. Box 66919 Los Angeles, CA 90099-5925	Daily Graphs	50 and 200 days

Company Name and Address	Chart Series	Length of Moving Averages
Securities Research 101 Prescott St. Wellesley Hills, MA 02181-3319	21-Month Security Charts	65 and 195 days
R.W. Mansfield 2973 Kennedy Blvd. Jersey City, NJ 07306	Weekly Charts on N.Y., AMEX, or Over-the-counter stocks	50 and 150 days

Figure 9.7
A PARABOLIC PRICE CURVE AND VARIOUS LENGTH MOVING AVERAGES

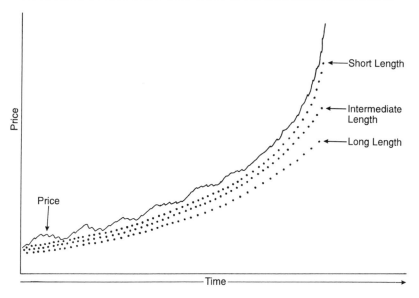

Figure 9.8
USE OF STOP LOSS ORDERS TO PROTECT PROFIT IN PARABOLIC PRICE CURVE

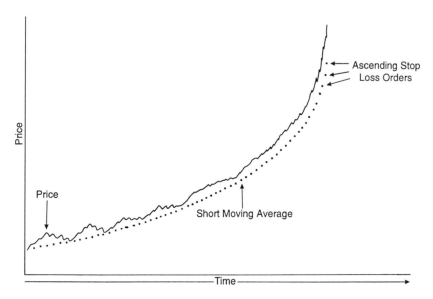

Chapter Ten
ACCUMULATION AND DISTRIBUTION

DEFINITION AND CHARACTERISTICS OF ACCUMULATION

Accumulation is the acquisition of a large number of shares of a stock by knowledgeable investors who intend to hold them for a major price rise. They place their offers to buy at the current price or at nearby prices to avoid pushing the price up prematurely. The more shares they accumulate, the fewer are available to others who wish to buy, and the available supply shrinks relative to demand. As this imbalance increases, the upward pressure grows until the price begins to move higher.

This process takes from several weeks to a year or more. The amount of time required depends on the amount of stock available for purchase and on the pace at which they can be acquired without bidding the price up a large amount. If the supply of stock is very large, it takes a long time to accumulate a significant amount. The process of accumulation is therefore most effective on companies with less than 25,000,000 shares, where it can have the intended impact in a few weeks or months.

The largest amount of accumulation occurs at major bottoms. However, some accumulation may occur during any stage of the market and at any price level between the bottom and the top. Thus some accumulation may occur during uptrends and within continuation patterns.

Awareness of the accumulation tactics of the well-informed investors enables you to make a better assessment of the potential for a stock to make a major long-term move upward. There are two situations in which it is most advantageous to know that a stock is under accumulation. One is when a stock is making a rounding bottom. The other is when a stock has been in a trading range.

Signs of Accumulation

ACCUMULATION WITHIN A ROUNDING BOTTOM

The formation of a rounding bottom is usually an extended process. (See Figure 10.1.) The decline in the price gradually decelerates until it merges into a section of the bottom which is almost flat which then merges into a gradually accelerating rise. Because the initial phase of the price rise is so slow, the complete outline of the rounding bottom does not become apparent until an uptrend has been established. If you can detect an accumulation process in a price pattern which could become a rounding bottom, you can be more confident that the price will eventually develop an uptrend.

ACCUMULATION WITHIN A TRADING RANGE

When a trading range forms, there is uncertainty about whether the price breakout will be to the upside or the downside. If well-informed, long-term investors are buying within the trading range, the eventual breakout will probably be to the upside. But you should not buy the stock until the breakout occurs, because the upside breakout is not a certainty, and the length of a trading range can't be determined in advance. (See Figure 10.2.)

INFORMATION ON ACCUMULATION DATA

Investor's Business Daily prints accumulation ratings on each stock it lists for the New York and American Exchanges and for the National Association of Dealers Automated Quote (NASDAQ) system. This newspaper reviews the transactions in each stock daily and provides a rating of A or B if the stock is being accumulated. An A rating for accumulation is the strongest rating. The B rating is not as strong and a C is neutral. This newspaper is available in some libraries and brokers' offices. A subscription is available from *Investor's Daily* main office at 12655 Beatrice Street, Los Angeles, CA 90066. Telephone: 1-800-521-8300.

FLOATING SUPPLY OF COMMON STOCK

The supply of shares available for purchase is called the floating supply. The number of floating shares can be estimated from the figures in the *Standard and Poor's* sheet available in brokerage offices and public libraries. On the back of that sheet, the total number of common shares is indicated under the heading "Capitalization."

The shares listed under this heading may be thought of in four separate categories:

- Issued shares: This is the total number of shares which have been issued by the corporation. This quantity is the same as that indicated under "Capitalization."

Figure 10.1
ACCUMULATION DURING A ROUNDING BOTTOM

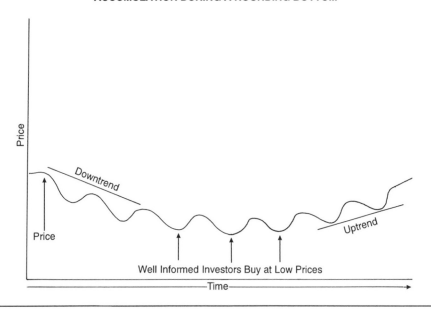

Figure 10.2
ACCUMULATION IN A TRADING RANGE

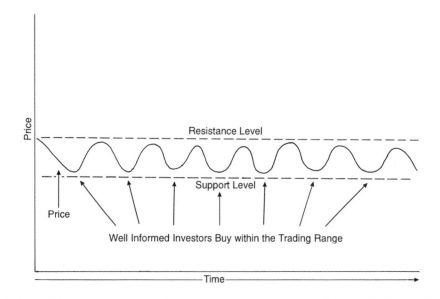

- Outstanding shares: Only those shares which are released from the corporation treasury are outstanding. Some companies retain a portion of the issued shares in the treasury to be available for stock option plans, acquisitions, etc.

- Closely held shares: Of the outstanding shares, some are held by organizations such as funds or major stockholders who want to maintain a long-term ownership in the corporation and do not intend to trade them in the foreseeable future.

- Floating supply (commonly referred to as the float). These are the shares held by the general public, short-term traders, speculators, and other individuals or organizations who think of themselves as temporary owners willing to sell their shares when they appear to be overpriced or when they decide to take their profits (or losses). By subtracting the closely held shares from the quantity outstanding, you arrive at the number of shares in the float.

Large blocks of shares held by officers in the company or by mutual funds become part of the float if they are sold on the open market. Often large block trades are transacted by prearrangement—from one large block holder to another—and reported to an exchange for display to the public.

Note: Figures on the number of outstanding shares and the float are updated weekly and displayed in the charts published by Daily Graphs, P.O. Box 66919, Los Angeles, CA 90099-5925.

DEFINITION AND CHARACTERISTICS OF DISTRIBUTION

Distribution is the process by which the most knowledgeable investors sell their shares to the general public, to less informed speculators, and to others willing to pay top prices. After a long rise in the price, those well informed investors conclude the price of a stock is about to start a major decline. They sell their shares while the stock is forming the top. They offer their shares at current or nearby prices so as not to push the price down while they are selling.

DISTRIBUTION WITHIN A ROUNDING TOP

The high volume of trading during tops provides the best situation for the distribution of the large quantities of shares held by distributors. Because a rounding top usually takes some time to complete itself, the distributors can sell their large holdings piecemeal in small quantities, so as not to depress the price. (See Figures 10.3 and 10.4.) As the selling continues, the number of buyers gradually diminishes, because they see that the price is no longer rising. Eventually, this weakening demand results in lower prices and a major decline begins.

Figure 10.3
DISTRIBUTION DURING A ROUNDING TOP

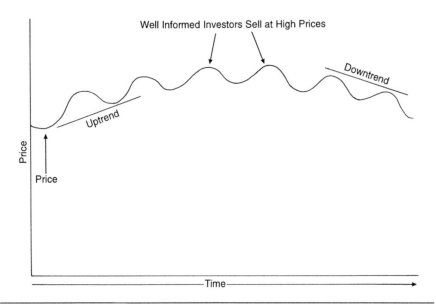

Figure 10.4
DISTRIBUTION IN A TRADING RANGE

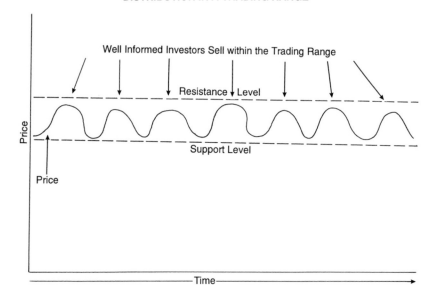

RELATIONSHIP BETWEEN DISTRIBUTION
AND FLOATING SUPPLY

Distribution usually takes less time than accumulation, because buyers are eager to own a stock which has been rising. The time required depends on the pace at which the distribution can be accomplished at the prevailing prices. The floating supply increases during distribution as some holders of large blocks (sometimes including company officials) sell all or part of their holdings. As the supply increases and the demand for the shares decreases, the downward pressure on the price exerts itself and the stock begins to decline.

DISTRIBUTION WITHIN A TRADING RANGE

If a stock you are holding goes into a trading range, you should determine if distribution is occurring. If you detect this process, you have an early warning that the price may be about to decline. However, a stock which enters a trading range after a rise in price is not necessarily being distributed. Instead, some trading ranges provide the opportunity for additional accumulation, and the price rise continues after a breakout to the upside. Being able to distinguish between trading ranges which are continuation patterns during a long-term price rise and those where distribution is occurring provides you with valuable insight.

INFORMATION ON DISTRIBUTION DATA

Information on distribution data is printed in *Investor's Business Daily*. Stocks which are given the rating of D or E are under distribution. An E rating is the strongest rating for distribution and a consistent E rating usually accompanies a faster breakthrough of a support level or a quicker completion of a rounding top. The D rating is not as strong. With either rating, though, the stock price becomes vulnerable to a decline.

When you detect persistent distribution, you should be prepared to sell. If your stock is being distributed within a trading range, you can sell it with more confidence even if the penetration of the support level is on medium or low volume.

Reliability of Accumulation and Distribution Data

Data on accumulation and distribution become more reliable with stronger ratings. Some examples:

- A continuous accumulation rating of A is more reliable than one which slips to a B rating at various times.

IBD

A,B = Accumulation   Price

D,E = Distribution

- An A rating for accumulation recurring daily for six months straight would be more reliable than one that lasted fewer months and then declined to a B rating.

- An A rating for the first month followed by a B rating for the second month, followed by an A rating for the third month, followed by a B rating for the fourth month would be more reliable than a B rating for four consecutive months.

- A continuous E rating for distribution is more reliable than one which changes to a D rating at various times.

- An E rating for distribution recurring daily for six months straight would be more reliable than one that lasted fewer months and then changed to a D rating.

- An E rating for the first month followed by a D rating for the second month, followed by an E rating for the third month, followed by a D rating for the fourth month would be more reliable than a D rating for four consecutive months.

ACCUMULATION EXERCISE

The following exercise provides the opportunity to insure your understanding of the concept of accumulation. Review the six pairs of data which follow. For each pair of stocks, information on accumulation and the float is provided. Place a check beside the stock you believe is the better one to buy. If neither one is better, don't check either. After giving your answers, check them in Appendix A.

Exercise Questions

Pair #1
  Stock #1 ___6 months of A rated accumulation.
        Float: 10,000,000 shares.
  Stock #2 ___6 months of C rated accumulation.
        Float: 100,000,000 shares.
Pair #2
  Stock #1 ___8 months of A rated accumulation.
        Float: 50,000,000 shares.
  Stock #2 ___8 months of B rated accumulation.
        Float: 50,000,000 shares.
Pair #3
  Stock #1 ___7 months of C rated accumulation.
        Float: 5,000,000 shares.
  Stock #2 ___7 months of B rated accumulation.
        Float: 10,000,000 shares.

Pair #4
   Stock #1 ___1 year of A rated accumulation.
      Float: 40,000,000 shares.
   Stock #2 ___1 year of A rated accumulation.
      Float: 50,000,000 shares.
Pair #5
   Stock #1 ___6 months of A rated accumulation.
      Float: 500,000,000 shares.
   Stock #2 ___6 months of B rated accumulation.
      Float: 5,000,000 shares.
Pair #6
   Stock #1 ___1 year of C rated accumulation.
      Float: 100,000,000 shares.
   Stock #2 ___1 year of C rated accumulation.
      Float: 50,000,000 shares.

DISTRIBUTION EXERCISE

The following exercise provides the opportunity to insure your understanding of the concept of distribution. Review the six pairs of stocks which follow. For each pair, information on distribution ratings and the number of shares outstanding is provided. Unless otherwise stated, the number of shares in the floating supply is equal for both stocks. Also, assume that the demand for each stock is equal.

Place a check beside the stock you feel is most susceptible to a decline in price. If you decide that neither stock has a higher susceptibility, don't check either one. See Appendix A for answers.

Exercise Questions

Pair #1
   Stock #1 ___Six months of E rated distribution.
      Outstanding shares: 10,000,000.
   Stock #2 ___Six months of a C rating.
      Outstanding shares: 10,000,000.
Pair #2
   Stock #1 ___Eight months of E rated distribution.
      Outstanding shares: 50,000,000.
   Stock #2 ___Eight months of D rated distribution.
      Outstanding shares: 50,000,000.
Pair #3
   Stock #1 ___Six months of E rated distribution.
      Outstanding shares: 100,000,000.
   Stock #2 ___One year of E rated distribution.

        Outstanding shares: 100,000,000.
Pair #4
    Stock #1 ___One year of a C rating.
        Outstanding shares: 300,000,000.
    Stock #2 ___One year of a C rating.
        Outstanding shares: 100,000,000.
Pair #5
    Stock #1 ___One year of E rated distribution.
        Outstanding shares: 50,000,000.
        Float at beginning of the year: 40,000,000.
    Stock #2 ___One year of D rated distribution.
        Outstanding shares: 50,000,000.
        Float at beginning of the year: 40,000,000.
Pair #6
    Stock #1 ___One year of D rated distribution.
        Outstanding shares: 50,000,000.
        Float at beginning of the year: 40,000,000.
    Stock #2 ___One year of D rated distribution.
        Outstanding shares: 50,000,000.
        Float at beginning of the year: 30,000,000.

In the preceding exercises the time periods of accumulation and distribution were clearly defined by months or years. Actual ratings may fluctuate erratically. The ratings can change daily. They can skip from any rating to any other rating. A rating can stay the same for several months and then change to another rating for a few days and then back again, etc. Thus, there is no restriction on how or when the ratings can change. The ideal situation is to find a stock where the rating is consistently an A or an E until the price starts to move in reflection of that rating. The general rule is that the more consistent rating leads to a greater reliability.

Chapter Eleven

INTERPRETING TECHNICAL INDICATORS

The purpose of this chapter is to help you develop the ability to interpret stock charts which show price patterns and trends, volume of trading, and moving averages. There are two sections in this chapter. One deals with making decisions about buying or rejecting stocks and the other with holding or selling stocks.

It's relative easy to make a decision when all indicators are in agreement. But there are many times when they are not unanimous. This chapter provides opportunities to practice decision-making in both situations in simulation exercises.

INTERPRETING TECHNICAL INDICATORS

The first step is to evaluate the price and volume action. Look for a breakout above a resistance level or the beginning of an uptrend on increased volume. Either of these events indicates the stock has potential for a capital gain. Second, check the moving average to see if it has been penetrated to the upside by the price. If so, this confirms the significance of the price and volume action.

Third, check *Investor's Business Daily* or another source of accumulation data. Look for a consistently high record of accumulation in the preceding weeks, months, or years. The higher the rating and the longer it has persisted, the more reliable the information. When you find a stock which has all these indicators in agreement, it may be selected for purchase.

In most cases, however, the indicators will not be in total agreement. To assess the potential in a stock on which the indicators disagree, use the following guidelines:

1. If the weight of the evidence is positive and convincing, you may buy the stock.

2. If the weight of evidence is positive but not convincing and you believe the potential gain is large, wait for more information.

3.   If the weight of the evidence is negative, reject the stock.

The following examples provide opportunities for you to confirm your ability to apply these guidelines and decide whether to buy, wait for more information, or reject the stock and look elsewhere.

Interpretation Exercise: Buy, Wait, or Reject?

Example 1. See Figure 11.1.

Information Available

Price/volume action: The price has just broken out from a trading range with a large increase in trading volume.

Moving average: The intermediate average has been penetrated to the upside.

Accumulation/distribution: Accumulation at a high rate has been underway for a more than a year.

Float: This is small, less than 10 million shares.

Interpretation

The extended accumulation period is an indication that knowledgeable long-term investors have been buying. A price breakout above the resistance level of the trading range on high volume is the main reason to purchase this stock. The penetration of the intermediate moving average to the upside is an additional positive factor.

Conclusion

This stock can be bought now with the hope for a major rise.

Example 2. See Figure 11.2.

Information Available

Price/volume action: The price could be making a rounding bottom or fluctuating within a trading range. The volume has dropped.

Moving average: The price is below the long moving average.

Accumulation/distribution: No evidence of accumulation or distribution.

Float: 800 million shares.

Interpretation

The current low volume, lack of accumulation, and the position of the price below the long average are all negative indications. The unknown factor is whether it will bottom out or settle into a trading range. Even if an accumulation process started, it would be a long time with the high number of shares before it would have any effect.

Conclusion

The prospective buyer of this stock faces the typical issue presented by a stock which has declined a long way. The low price is tempting, but is there a good

Figure 11.1
BUY, WAIT, OR REJECT?

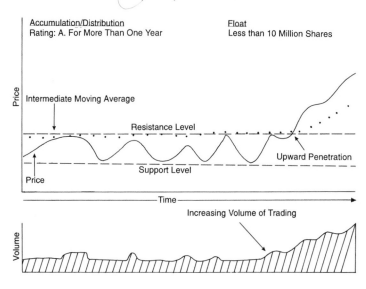

Figure 11.2
BUY, WAIT, OR REJECT?

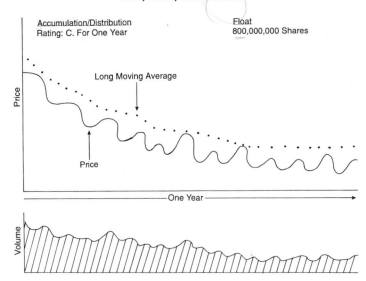

reason to believe it won't remain low? In this case, there is no reason to be optimistic. Reject this one.

Example 3. See Figure 11.3.

Information Available

Price/volume action: The stock has been in a wide long trading range and has been close to the top of the range for several weeks.

Moving average: An intermediate average has been penetrated to the upside.

Accumulation/distribution: Accumulation has been occurring at a slow pace.

Float: Less than 10 million shares.

Interpretation

The stock appears to be ready for a breakout to the upside, but the point at which this will happen is uncertain. It is a positive sign that the price has been near the top of the range recently and could indicate the supply is diminishing relative to the demand. Penetration of the intermediate average is another encouraging sign.

Conclusion

The evidence in this case is positive, but insufficient to warrant a purchase until an upside breakout from the trading range develops. If that happens, the evidence to support buying this stock would be convincing and the potential profit large. It is worth waiting for this one.

Example 4. See Figure 11.4.

Information Available

Price/volume action: The stock has broken through the resistance level of a trading range. The volume increased an insignificant amount during the breakout.

Moving average: The stock is still below its intermediate average.

Accumulation/distribution: There is evidence of a low rate of accumulation for two months.

Float: More than 100 million shares.

Interpretation

The breakout above resistance had insufficient volume to be convincing and raises doubt about its significance. It might have been caused by a rumor. If it was caused by a rumor and the rumor turns out to be false, the price would probably come back into the trading range. There has been only a short period of accumulation as compared to the large floating supply. Another negative factor is that the price is below its intermediate average.

Figure 11.3
BUY, WAIT, OR REJECT?

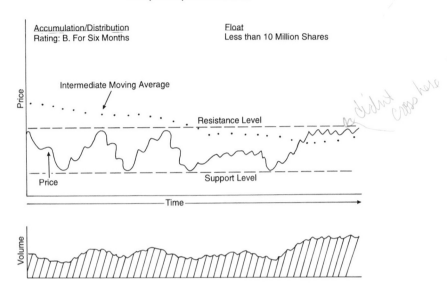

Figure 11.4
BUY, WAIT, OR REJECT?

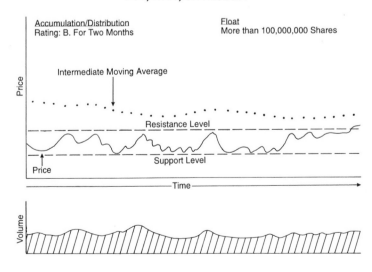

Conclusion

Reject this one. There's too much negative evidence.

Example 5. See Figure 11.5.

Information Available

Price/volume action: The price is trending downward slowly on low volume.

Moving average: The intermediate average is above the price and is tracking its descent.

Accumulation/distribution: There is no evidence of accumulation in this stock which has the neutral C rating.

Float: Above 100 million.

Interpretation

All the evidence is negative. The price is in a downtrend. The absence of accumulation and the small volume are signs of lack of interest by substantial investors and speculators. The large floating supply dampens the prospects for a rise in price. The intermediate moving average confirms the downtrend.

Conclusion

Reject this one. Let it drift lower without you.

Example 6. See Figure 11.6.

Information Available

Price/volume action: The price has made an upside penetration of the resistance level on increased volume. The price is now in an uptrend and volume is increasing.

Moving average: It was penetrated to the upside three months ago.

Accumulation/distribution: High pace of accumulation for nine months, followed by a slow pace for the next three months.

Float: Less than 15 million.

Interpretation

The simultaneous upside penetration of the resistance level and the moving average is very positive. The slow angle of ascent adds another positive element, because a slow rise (between 25 and 35 degrees) is more sustainable over the long term. Slow accumulation occurring within an uptrend is positive. Most of the accumulation would have been done at lower price levels.

Conclusion

Buy this one for a long-term gain. A slow steady rise portends good probability for large capital gains.

Figure 11.5
BUY, WAIT, OR REJECT?

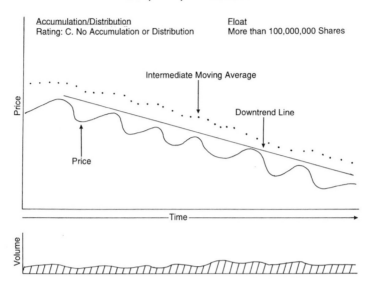

Figure 11.6
BUY, WAIT, OR REJECT?

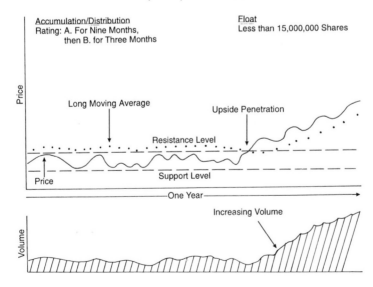

Example 7. See Figure 11.7.

Information Available

Price/volume action: This is a low-priced stock which has been fluctuating within a narrow trading range for two years. The volume is extremely low.

Moving average: The price has been criss-crossing its long average within the trading range.

Accumulation/distribution: Neutral rating.

Float: More than 100 million shares.

Interpretation

With no sign of accumulation or distribution and a large floating supply, this stock could remain in its trading range for years. The narrowness of the trading range and low trading volume within the range indicate lack of interest by both buyers and sellers.

Conclusion

Don't buy a low-priced stock, because it seems like a bargain. If other investors are not attracted by the price, there's probably good reason. The criss-crossing of the moving average reinforces the impression of indecision and lack of investor interest. This type of situation can waste your time. There is nothing positive here and this stock should be rejected.

Example 8. See Figure 11.8.

Information Available

Price/volume action: The price has just broken out above a resistance level and started on a steep uptrend on increasing volume.

Moving average: The long average has been penetrated to the upside.

Accumulation/distribution: This stock has been under accumulation at a low rate for one and a half years, followed by a high rate for six months.

Float: Less than 5 million shares.

Interpretation

This stock has a good profile for a large percent gain. High accumulation rate, small floating supply, sharp price increase accompanied by a sudden surge in trading volume, and upside penetration of both the moving average and the long-standing resistance level are promising signs.

Conclusion

Buy this one at the market in the hope for a significant percentage profit.

Example 9. See Figure 11.9.

Information Available

Price/volume action: The price has been in a trading range for the last year. Recently, the volume has been low, and the price has been unable to rise above the middle of the range.

Figure 11.7
BUY, WAIT, OR REJECT?

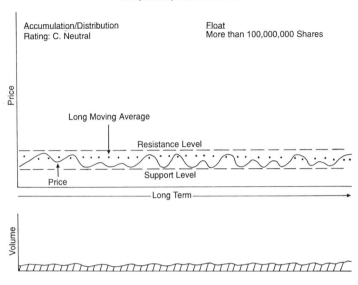

Figure 11.8
BUY, WAIT, OR REJECT?

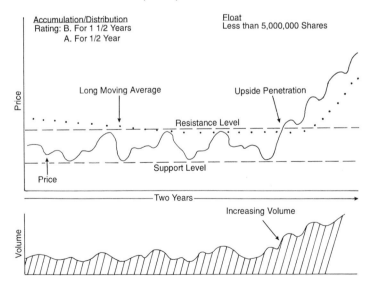

Figure 11.9
BUY, WAIT, OR REJECT?

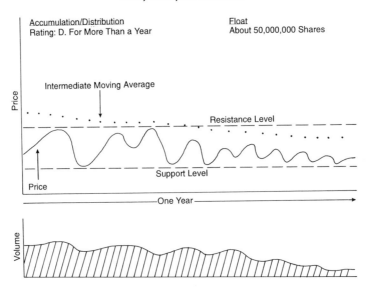

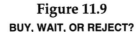

Moving average: The price is below the intermediate average.

Accumulation/distribution: There has been evidence of slow distribution for more than one year.

Float: About 50 million shares.

Interpretation

This situation is negative. Declining price and volume are evidence of lack of buyer interest. The persistent distribution indicates knowledgeable investors have been selling. Any breakout will probably be to the down side, since both the price and the volume have been weak.

Conclusion

Reject this one.

Example 10. See Figure 11.10.

Information Available

Price/volume action: The price has been in a wide trading range for the last year. During this time, the volume has risen when the stock rose and declined as it fell.

Moving average: The intermediate moving average is just below the resistance level of the trading range.

Figure 11.10
BUY, WAIT, OR REJECT?

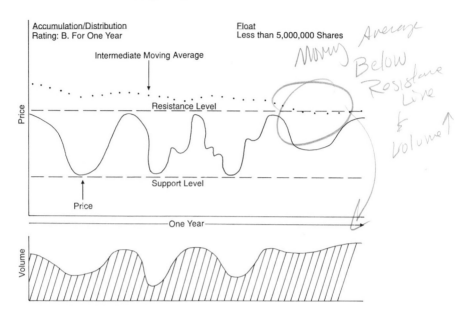

Accumulation/distribution: This stock has been accumulated at a slow pace for the last year.

Float: Less than 5 million shares.

Interpretation

This stock provides a good opportunity for a patient investor. There is a small floating supply which has been under accumulation for a year. The rising volume accompanying price increases and declining volume accompanying price decreases have positive implications.

Conclusion

The slow but consistent accumulation and the small floating supply promise profits to the patient. If the price breaks up through the resistance level, buy "at the market."

Example 11. See Figure 11.11.

Information Available

Price/volume action: This pattern gives the appearance of a rounding bottom which has yet to develop an identifiable uptrend. The volume has been increasing for the last six months.

   Moving average: The price has almost reached the long moving average.

   Accumulation/distribution: Accumulation has been occurring at a fast pace for the last six months after a B rating for the previous six months.

   Float: Less than 5 million.

Interpretation

The increase in the pace of accumulation and the small floating supply are the most positive aspects of this situation. If the rounding bottom completes itself and an uptrend develops, this could be a good opportunity for a major capital gain.

Conclusion

Wait for this one. When the moving average is penetrated and an uptrend is formed, buy it.

Figure 11.11
BUY, WAIT, OR REJECT?

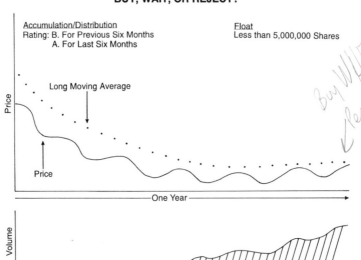

HOLD OR SELL DECISION GUIDELINES

When you are holding a stock, you are in a continuous decision process of deciding how long to hold and when to sell. Here are some guidelines to help you decide:

1. If the price is in an uptrend and above the uptrend line or its long moving average, hold. (You will see one exception to this guideline in Example 21 and the accompanying figure.)
2. If the price is within a triangle, rectangle, or trading range, hold.
3. If the price has penetrated both the trend line and the long moving average, sell.
4. If the price has penetrated the bottom line of a triangle, rectangle, or trading range, and the long moving average, sell.
5. If the price goes into a downtrend, sell if the long moving average is penetrated to the downside.
6. If two indicators are in direct conflict, use the weight of evidence provided by the remaining indicators to make the hold or sell decision. Sell if the weight of evidence is negative. Hold if it is positive. When the evidence is balanced and you are uncertain, hold.

General Comment

A long-term buy and hold investment strategy has the advantages of large capital gains and fewer commissions. The short-term approach often results in small profits, many commissions, more headaches, and extra paperwork. In the worst case, short-term investors churn their own accounts and help their brokers become rich while they see their own capital shrink.

Interpretation Exercise: Hold or Sell?

Example 12. See Figure 11.12.

Information Available

Price/volume action: The volume of trading for the past two months has been heavy. It increased when the uptrend line was penetrated to the downside. The price has formed a downtrend.

Moving average: The long moving average has been penetrated to the downside.

Accumulation/distribution: This stock has been distributed at a fast rate for two months.

Outstanding shares: The number of shares outside of those held in the company treasury is over 500 million.

Figure 11.12
HOLD OR SELL?

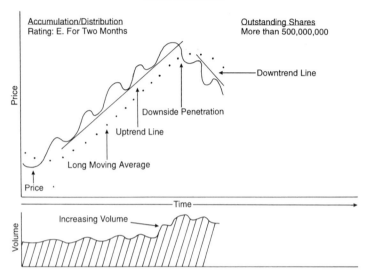

HOLD OR SELL?

Interpretation

There is plenty of negative evidence: fast distribution, penetration of the uptrend line and moving average, and heavy volume at the beginning of a downtrend. In addition, the large supply of shares suggests that there will be many potential sellers as the price declines.

Conclusion

Sell this one "at the market."

Example 13. See Figure 11.13.

Information Available

Price/volume action: The uptrend line was penetrated several months ago. Since then the price has continued upward at a lower angle of ascent. The volume of trading is medium.

> *Moving average:* The long moving average has not been penetrated.
> *Accumulation/distribution:* This stock has a rating of neutral C.
> *Outstanding shares:* Less than 10 million.

Interpretation

The weight of evidence is positive. A new uptrend has developed at a more sustainable angle of ascent. There hasn't been any distribution. The moving average has not been penetrated.

Figure 11.13
HOLD OR SELL?

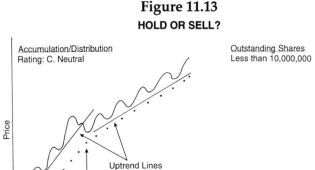

Accumulation/Distribution
Rating: C. Neutral

Outstanding Shares
Less than 10,000,000

Uptrend Lines

Long Moving Average

Price

Price

Time

Volume

Conclusion

Hold this stock and ride the new uptrend.

Example 14. See Figure 11.14.

Information Available

Price/volume action: The price has pulled away from the uptrend line and has begun to round over. The volume of trading has risen from low to medium.

    Moving average: The long moving average has not been penetrated.

    Accumulation/distribution: This stock has a B accumulation rating.

    Outstanding shares: More than 100 million.

Interpretation

The evidence is positive. The moving average and the uptrend line have not been penetrated. There is some accumulation occurring. The rounding over price action may or may not develop into a rounding top.

Conclusion

Hold the stock in the hope for additional gains, but be alert to signs of a possible rounding top, e.g., a switch to distribution or heavy volume accompanied by a stalling out of price gains.

Figure 11.14
HOLD OR SELL?

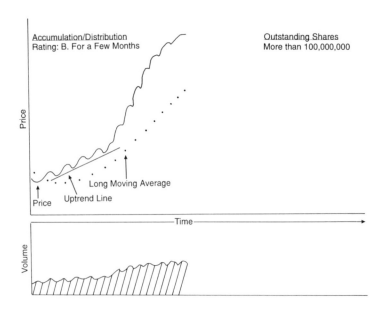

Accumulation/Distribution
Rating: B. For a Few Months

Outstanding Shares
More than 100,000,000

Price

Long Moving Average

Price   Uptrend Line

Time

Volume

Example 15. See Figure 11.15.

Information Available

Price/volume action: The price was in a steep uptrend on high volume. The uptrend line has been penetrated and the price is now in a symmetrical triangle. Within the triangle, the volume is declining.

> *Moving average:* The long moving average has not been penetrated.
> *Accumulation/distribution:* This stock has a B rating for the last two months.
> *Outstanding shares:* There are less than 10 million shares outstanding.

Interpretation

Except for the penetration of the trend line, there are no other negatives. The symmetrical triangle could become a short continuation pattern. Steep uptrends tend to have short life spans, and the resolution of the symmetrical triangle may be another uptrend with a lower angle of ascent. The accumulation rating of B gives reason to hope the breakout will be upward.

Conclusion

Hold, and hope for an upside breakout from the triangle.

Figure 11.15
HOLD OR SELL?

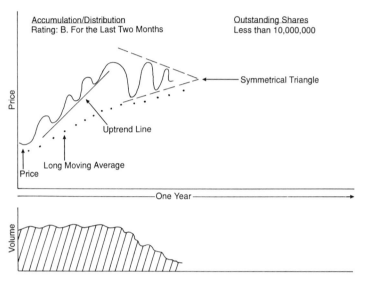

Accumulation/Distribution
Rating: B. For the Last Two Months

Outstanding Shares
Less than 10,000,000

Symmetrical Triangle

Uptrend Line

Long Moving Average

Price

Price

One Year

Volume

Example 16. See Figure 11.16.

Information Available

Price/volume action: The uptrend line was broken several months ago, and the price has been in a rectangle since then. For the most part, the price has been close to the top of the rectangle. The volume has diminished within the rectangle.

   Moving average: The long moving average has not been penetrated.

   Accumulation/distribution: This stock has had an A rating for three months.

   Outstanding shares: The quantity is less than 10 million.

Interpretation

The weight of evidence is positive. The price is demonstrating strength by staying close to the top of the rectangle. The fast pace of accumulation is another positive sign. The significance of the penetration of the uptrend line is questionable, because the moving average has not been penetrated.

Conclusion

Hold this stock, and hope for an upside breakout and the start of a new uptrend.

Figure 11.16
HOLD OR SELL?

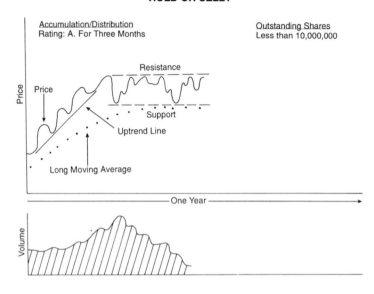

Accumulation/Distribution
Rating: A. For Three Months

Outstanding Shares
Less than 10,000,000

Resistance

Price

Price

Support

Uptrend Line

Long Moving Average

One Year

Volume

Example 17. See Figure 11.17.

Information Available

Price/volume action: Two months ago, the price broke through an uptrend line on low volume, at which point, an ascending triangle developed. The volume has been diminishing within the triangle.

Moving average: The long moving average has not been penetrated.

Accumulation/distribution: The distribution rating switched from a C rating to a B rating two months ago.

Outstanding shares: There are less than 10 million shares outstanding.

Interpretation

The ascending triangle and the accumulation within it are positive signs. Since the moving average has not been penetrated, there is reason to hope for further price gains.

Conclusion

Hold this stock, and hope for a breakout to the upside of the triangle and the development of another uptrend. If the price drops through the bottom of the triangle and the moving average, sell.

Figure 11.17
HOLD OR SELL?

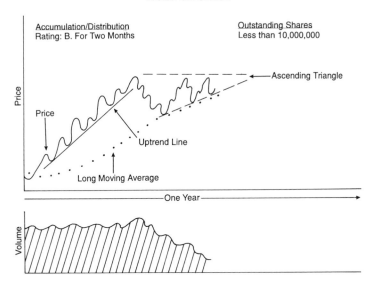

Accumulation/Distribution
Rating: B. For Two Months

Outstanding Shares
Less than 10,000,000

Ascending Triangle

Price

Price

Uptrend Line

Long Moving Average

One Year

Volume

Example 18. See Figure 11.18.

Information Available

Price/volume action: A long-term uptrend has been penetrated to the downside. The volume remains moderate.

Moving average: The long average has not been penetrated by the price decline.

Accumulation/distribution: The rating has been fluctuating between B and D.

Outstanding shares: There are less than 10 million outstanding.

Interpretation

The penetration of the uptrend is a negative indication. But long-term up-trends are frequently interrupted by short-term declines. The significance of this decline will be determined by whether or not it penetrates the moving average.

Conclusion

Hold the stock until the moving average is penetrated to the downside.

Figure 11.18
HOLD OR SELL?

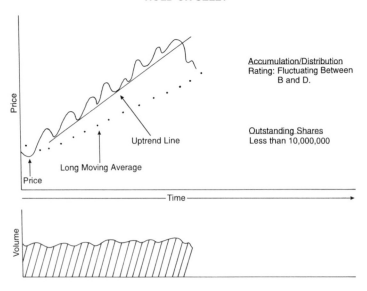

Example 19. See Figure 11.19.

Information Available

Price/volume action: After a long rise in the price, a potential rounding top is half complete. The uptrend line has been penetrated on medium volume.

 Moving average: The long moving average has not been penetrated.

 Accumulation/distribution: The rating has gone from B to D.

 Outstanding shares: There are less than 10 million shares outstanding.

Interpretation

The penetration of the uptrend line and the switch to distribution are negative signs. The medium volume of trading is positive since tops are usually made on high volume. No penetration of the long moving average is a positive sign. The weight of evidence is balanced.

Conclusion

Hold the stock, and hope the distribution stops and a new uptrend develops. To protect your large capital gain, be prepared to sell if the moving average is penetrated to the downside.

Figure 11.19
HOLD OR SELL?

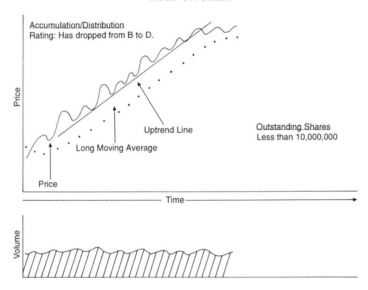

Example 20. See Figure 11.20.

Information Available

Price/volume action: The price has broken through the uptrend line and is in a descending triangle. The volume is low.

Moving average: The price is just above the long moving average, which is just below the bottom of the triangle.

Accumulation/distribution: This stock has been under fast distribution for three months.

Outstanding shares: Less than 10 million.

Interpretation

Holders of this stock should be wary. The implications of the fast distribution and the descending triangles are negative.

Conclusion

Since the moving average is not penetrated, hold but protect your profit by placing a stop loss order under the moving average.

Figure 11.20
HOLD OR SELL?

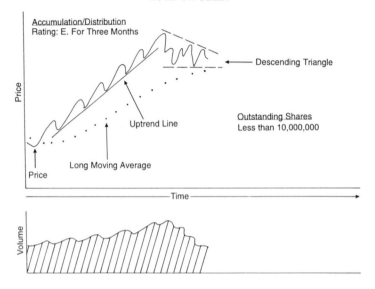

Example 21. See Figure 11.21.

Information Available

Price/volume action: The price is entering the vertical phase of a parabolic upward curve. The volume of trading has been extremely high for the last few weeks as the price skyrocketed.

   Moving average: The price has pulled well above the long moving average.

   Accumulation/distribution: This stock has switched from an A rating to an E rating.

   Outstanding shares: The number of shares outstanding is more than 200,000,000.

Interpretation

This is a parabolic upward curving price which "runs away" from the previous trend line and the long moving average. A relevant trend line can't be drawn because there are no bottoms in the latest section of the curve. The long moving average serves no useful purpose either, because it lags behind the current price too much. The high volume and the nonstop price rise are evidence of excessive speculation. The sudden switch from accumulation to fast distribution indicates long-term investors recognize the dangers of this type of speculation and are selling out.

Figure 11.21
HOLD OR SELL?

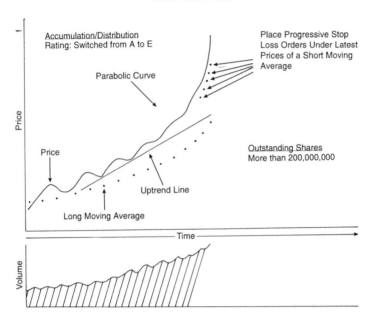

Accumulation/Distribution
Rating: Switched from A to E

Parabolic Curve

Price

Place Progressive Stop
Loss Orders Under Latest
Prices of a Short Moving
Average

Outstanding Shares
More than 200,000,000

Price

Uptrend Line

Long Moving Average

Time

Volume

Conclusion

You should also prepare to sell. Place a stop loss order under the latest price in a short moving average. Raise the selling price of the stop loss order each morning until it is activated, and you are sold out with your large profit.

Example 22. See Figure 11.22.

Information Available

Price/volume action: After a sustained rise for a year followed by a penetration of the uptrend line, the price formed a symmetrical triangle. Volume declined as the price formed the triangle and exited where the upper and lower boundary lines meet.

Moving average: The price is right at its long moving average.

Accumulation/distribution: The rating has been neutral for the last two months.

Outstanding shares: Less than 10 million.

Figure 11.22
HOLD OR SELL?

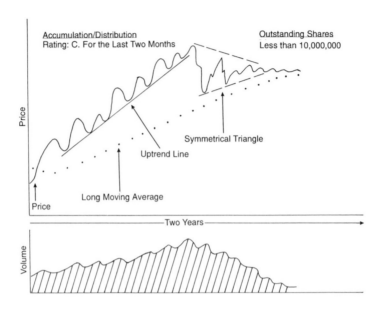

Interpretation

The last two months have been a power struggle between the buyers and the sellers which ended in a draw. This balance of power is reflected by the indicators, which are also in balance. Subsequent direction of the price will be determined by the next news on the company.

Conclusion

Hold this one, and hope the rise will resume. To protect your profit, place a stop loss order under the moving average.

INSTRUCTIONS FOR SIMULATION EXERCISE

In the following sections, you will have an opportunity to practice chart interpretations. Each of the charts is similar to one of those you have seen previously in this chapter. The difference is that the trend lines, resistance and support levels, and pattern interpretation are absent. You may wish to draw in the trend lines, resistance and support levels, triangle boundaries, etc., where you decide they should be.

The section which follows contains eleven charts for your interpretation. After reviewing each figure, decide whether you would buy now, wait for more information, or reject the stock outright. After making your decision, check each answer in Appendix A, Exercise Answers for Chapter 11, Figures 11E.1 through 11E.11.

The subsequent section contains eleven more charts for your interpretation. Assume that you now own each stock represented in the figures in this section. Decide whether you would continue to hold it or sell. Check each answer in Appendix A, Exercise Answers for Chapter 11, Figures 11E.12 through 11E.22.

SIMULATION EXERCISE

Section 1: Buy, Wait, or Reject?

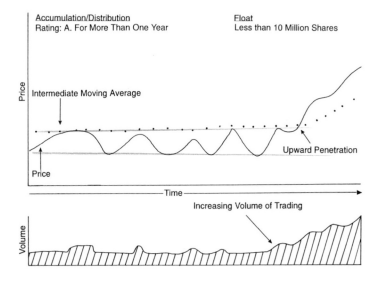

Figure 11E.1

BUY, WAIT, OR REJECT?

Figure 11E.2
BUY, WAIT, OR REJECT?

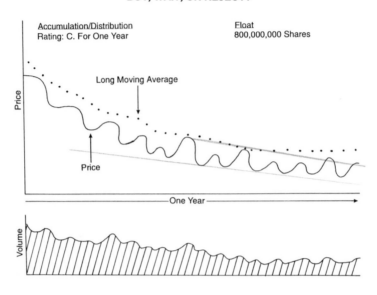

Figure 11E.3
BUY, WAIT, OR REJECT?

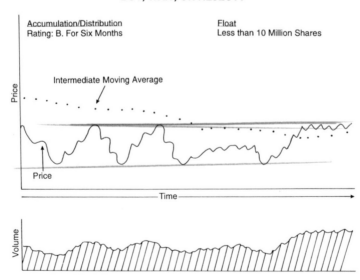

Figure 11E.4
BUY, WAIT, OR REJECT?

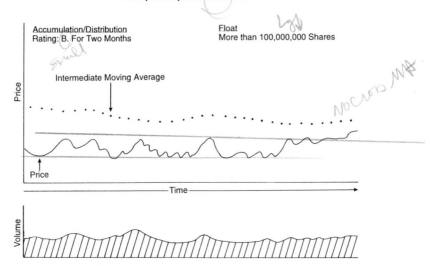

Accumulation/Distribution
Rating: B. For Two Months

Float
More than 100,000,000 Shares

Intermediate Moving Average

Price

Price

Time

Volume

Figure 11E.5
BUY, WAIT, OR REJECT?

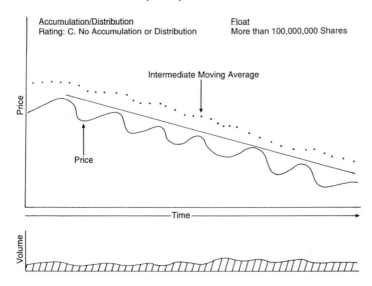

Accumulation/Distribution
Rating: C. No Accumulation or Distribution

Float
More than 100,000,000 Shares

Intermediate Moving Average

Price

Price

Time

Volume

Figure 11E.6
BUY, WAIT, OR REJECT?

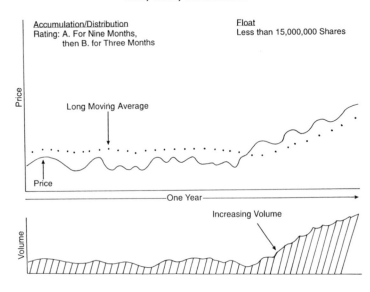

Accumulation/Distribution
Rating: A. For Nine Months,
then B. for Three Months

Float
Less than 15,000,000 Shares

Price

Long Moving Average

Price

One Year

Volume

Increasing Volume

Figure 11E.7
BUY, WAIT, OR REJECT?

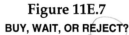

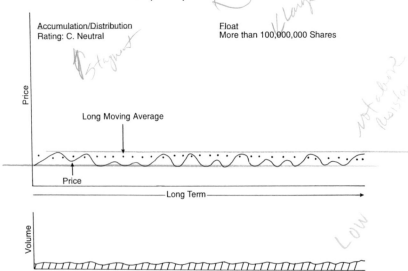

Accumulation/Distribution
Rating: C. Neutral

Float
More than 100,000,000 Shares

Price

Long Moving Average

Price

Long Term

Volume

Figure 11E.8
BUY, WAIT, OR REJECT?

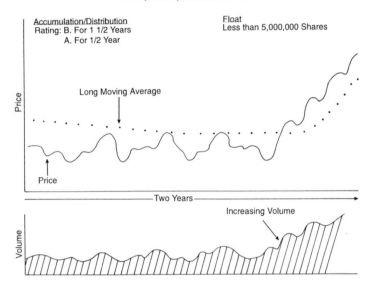

Figure 11E.9
BUY, WAIT, OR REJECT?

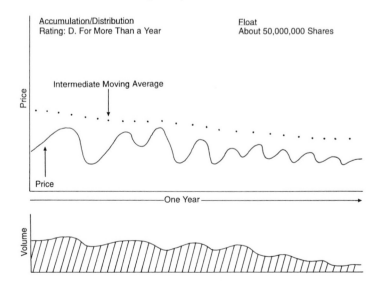

Figure 11E.10
BUY, WAIT, OR REJECT?

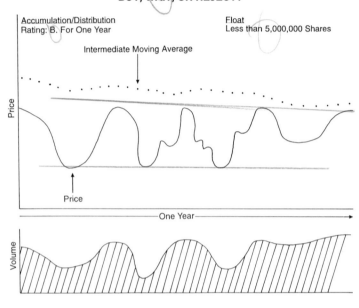

Accumulation/Distribution
Rating: B. For One Year

Float
Less than 5,000,000 Shares

Intermediate Moving Average

Price

Price

One Year

Volume

Figure 11E.11
BUY, WAIT, OR REJECT?

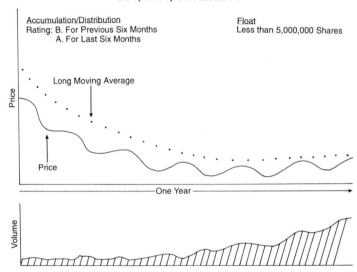

Accumulation/Distribution
Rating: B. For Previous Six Months
          A. For Last Six Months

Float
Less than 5,000,000 Shares

Long Moving Average

Price

Price

One Year

Volume

SIMULATION EXERCISE

Section 2: Hold or Sell?

Figure 11E.12
HOLD OR SELL?

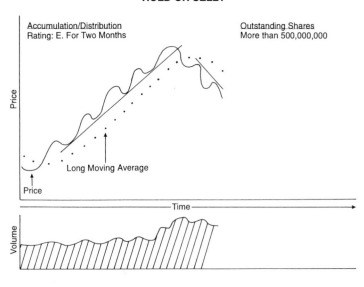

Figure 11E.13
HOLD OR SELL?

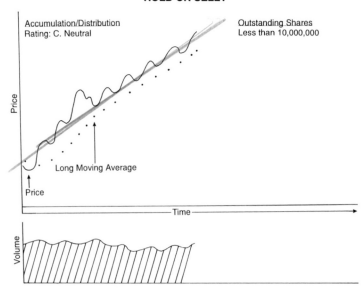

Accumulation/Distribution
Rating: C. Neutral

Outstanding Shares
Less than 10,000,000

Price

Long Moving Average

Price

Time

Volume

Figure 11E.14
HOLD OR SELL?

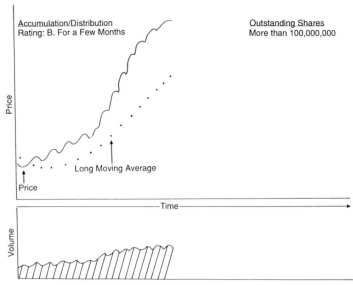

Accumulation/Distribution
Rating: B. For a Few Months

Outstanding Shares
More than 100,000,000

Price

Long Moving Average

Price

Time

Volume

Figure 11E.15
HOLD OR SELL?

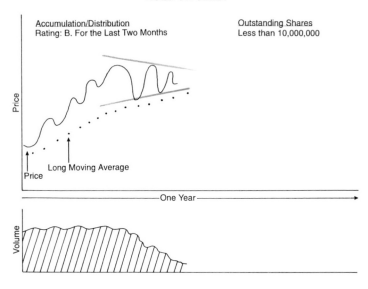

Accumulation/Distribution
Rating: B. For the Last Two Months

Outstanding Shares
Less than 10,000,000

Price

Long Moving Average

Price

One Year

Volume

Figure 11E.16
HOLD OR SELL?

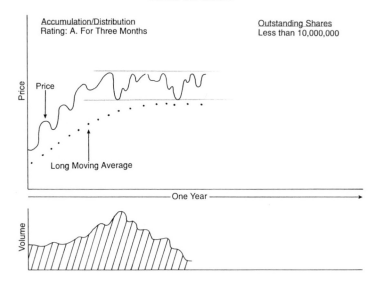

Accumulation/Distribution
Rating: A. For Three Months

Outstanding Shares
Less than 10,000,000

Price

Price

Long Moving Average

One Year

Volume

Figure 11E.17
HOLD OR SELL?

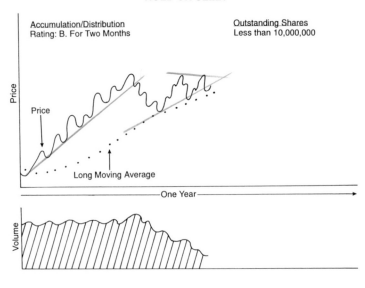

Accumulation/Distribution
Rating: B. For Two Months

Outstanding Shares
Less than 10,000,000

Price

Price

Long Moving Average

One Year

Volume

Figure 11E.18
HOLD OR SELL?

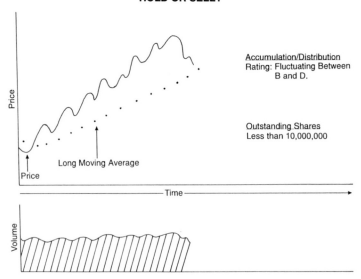

Price

Accumulation/Distribution
Rating: Fluctuating Between
B and D.

Outstanding Shares
Less than 10,000,000

Long Moving Average

Price

Time

Volume

Figure 11E.19
HOLD OR SELL?

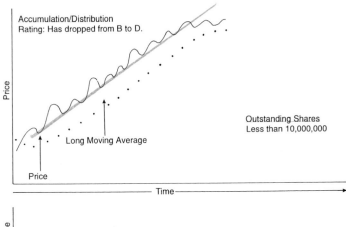

Accumulation/Distribution
Rating: Has dropped from B to D.

Price

Long Moving Average

Price

Outstanding Shares
Less than 10,000,000

Time

Volume

Figure 11E.20
HOLD OR SELL?

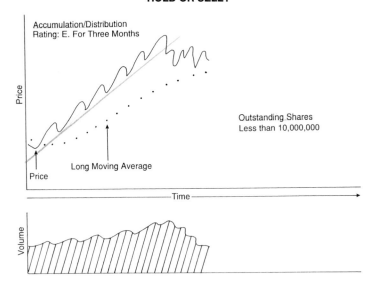

Accumulation/Distribution
Rating: E. For Three Months

Price

Long Moving Average

Price

Outstanding Shares
Less than 10,000,000

Time

Volume

Figure 11E.21
HOLD OR SELL?

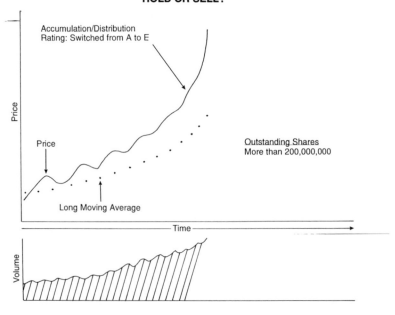

Accumulation/Distribution
Rating: Switched from A to E

Price

Price

Outstanding Shares
More than 200,000,000

Long Moving Average

Time

Volume

Figure 11E.22
HOLD OR SELL?

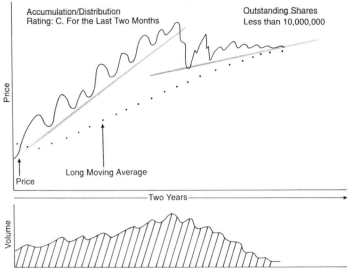

Accumulation/Distribution
Rating: C. For the Last Two Months

Outstanding Shares
Less than 10,000,000

Price

Price

Long Moving Average

Two Years

Volume

POSTSCRIPT

Nobody knows what the stock market or a particular stock will do in the future. You can use technical analysis to help you deal with this uncertainty. By analyzing information on accumulation and distribution, you can discover underlying buildup in buying or selling pressure. By reviewing price and volume, you can interpret price trends and changes in those trends. Moving averages provide the means to confirm or question those interpretations. These technical tools can reduce the level of uncertainty, but they can't eliminate it nor can they eliminate the risks involved.

When you analyze stock charts, you'll find some of them are open to more than one interpretation. Your ability to arrive at a reliable interpretation will increase as you gain experience. I recommend you confine your investments to small amounts until you satisfy yourself that your correct interpretations outnumber your erroneous ones. Finally, I wish you the best of good fortune in one of the most challenging endeavors—achieving success in the stock market.

Appendix A

EXERCISE ANSWERS

CHAPTER 2

Figure 2E.1. Yes. Since each bottom from C through I is higher than the preceding bottom, the uptrend is well defined.

Figure 2E.2. No. Although point C is higher than B, neither D nor E is higher than C, and a pattern of successively higher bottoms has not been established. Although the movement of the price from point E has gone above the preceding tops, the pattern of the tops does not define an uptrend; the pattern of the bottoms provides the definition.

Figure 2E.3. Yes. Although C is not higher than B, D, E, and F are a succession of higher bottoms, and an uptrend has therefore been established and confirmed.

Figure 2E.4. No. This pattern shows two attempts to establish an uptrend, neither of which was successful. Point B is higher than point A, but point C is lower than point B. Similarly, point E is higher than point D, but point F is lower than point E.

CHAPTER 3

Head-and-Shoulders Identification Exercise

Figure 3E.1. Yes. Point A is the left shoulder, point C is the head, and point E is the right shoulder. An upslanting neckline can be drawn through points B and D. This neckline was penetrated by the price as it declined from point E.

Figure 3E.2. Yes. Points A and E are the two shoulders, and point C is the head. A downslanting neckline can be drawn through points B and D, and this neckline was penetrated by the price as it declined from point E.

Figure 3E.3. Yes. Points A and E are the shoulders, with the head in the middle at point C. The upslanting neckline drawn through points B and D was penetrated by the price decline from point E.

Figure 3E.4. No. This price pattern does not qualify as a head and shoulders because the decline from point C stopped before it reached the level of point A. (The decline from the right side of the head must go lower than the top of the left shoulder to meet the criteria for the head-and-shoulders pattern.)

Double-Top Identification Exercise

Figure 3E.5. Yes. Points A and C form the two tops. Point B is the lowest price level in the valley floor, and that level was penetrated by the price decline from point C. Draw a horizontal line through point B and you will note that the final prices in the figure are below that line.

Figure 3E.6. Yes. Points A and C form the two tops. The final prices in the figure are below a horizontal line drawn through point B.

Figure 3E.7. Yes. Points A and C form the two tops at approximately the same level. The price rise from point D to point E did not go far enough to approximate the price level at point A or C. (If it had, it would have converted this double top into a triple-top price pattern that will be described in the following section.) The subsequent price decline from point E went below the price level at point B, which qualifies as a sell signal.

Figure 3E.8. No. Points A and C formed a potential double top, but the price rise from point D negated their significance by surpassing them by a considerable margin.

Triple-Top Identification Exercise

Figure 3E.9. Yes. Points A, C, and E represent the three tops. Point D is the lower of the two price levels for the valleys between the three tops. A horizontal line drawn through point D would be penetrated by the price decline from point E. A sell signal has therefore been given.

Figure 3E.10. No. The three points A, C, and E define a downtrend rather than a triple top. Top C is lower than top A, and top E is lower than top C; this relationship matches the definition of a downtrend.

Figure 3E.11. No. Top C is considerably higher than both top A and top E, so this price pattern qualifies as a head-and-shoulders formation rather than a triple top. A line drawn through points B and D would be penetrated by the price descent from point E, and this would complete the head-and-shoulders price pattern. Note that triple-top and head-and-shoulder price patterns have much the same significance. When completed, both patterns provide a strong sell signal and usually presage a significant decline in the price.

Figure 3E.12. Yes. This is an instance in which the tops are definitely not equidistant. However, they are approximately the same height, so the designation of triple top is justified. The sell signal is given when the price decline from point E penetrates the price level established at point B.

Rounding-Top Identification Exercise

Figures 3E.13–3E.15. Yes, for each. In each case, an uptrend on the left side of the chart is converted gradually into a downtrend on the right side of the chart. Between the uptrend and the downtrend the price trend is relatively flat, indicating a period of balance in the supply and demand for the stock. Note that the smoothness of the curve and the size of the price fluctuations that occur within the curve can vary considerably.

Figure 3E.16. No. Although this figure has an uptrend on the left side and a downtrend on the right side, it has two outstanding price peaks separated by an intervening valley. Since these price peaks occurred at the approximate same price level, the figure should be described as a double top.

Figure 3E.17. Yes. The uptrend on the left side of the figure is gradually converted to a downtrend on the right side.

Figure 3E.18. No. In this figure the uptrend on the left is not followed by a relatively flat top; it is followed by a downtrend. This is an example of an uptrend changing directly into a downtrend.

Descending-Triangle Identification Exercise

Figure 3E.19. Yes. Top C is lower than top A, and top E is lower than top C; a line drawn through these points will be descending. A line drawn through bottom points B, D, F, and G will meet the descending line to form a wedge, which in charting terms is referred to as a triangle. (The imaginary vertical third side of the triangle is not drawn because it is not needed to define the boundaries of the struggle between buyers and sellers.)

Figure 3E.20. Yes. Tops D, F, and G are each lower than the preceding tops; a line drawn through tops A, D, F, and G will descend to meet the horizontal line that can be drawn through bottoms B, C, E, H, and I. The wedge thus formed is referred to as a triangle.

Figure 3E.21. Yes. A line drawn through the tops will meet the line drawn through the bottoms. However, the price works its way out through the apex of this triangle and negates its significance.

Figure 3E.22. No. This is an uptrend changing directly into a downtrend. The uptrend is defined by the line that can be drawn through bottom points B, D, and F. The downtrend line can be drawn through tops E, G, I, K, and M.

CHAPTER 4

Downtrend Identification Exercise

Figure 4E.1. Yes. Each successive high from point C through point G is lower than the preceding highs. Tops A and B are at approximately the same level, so the downtrend was established by point C, confirmed by point D, and reconfirmed by points E, F, and G.

Figure 4E.2. No. While top C is lower than top B, top point D is not lower than top C. The development of a downtrend was not confirmed.

Figure 4E.3. Yes. Each of the successive top points in this figure is lower than the preceding points. A downtrend line can be drawn through top points B, C, D, and E. The top point F is considerably below that line, and this could signal the beginning of an accelerating downtrend.

Figure 4E.4. No. The downtrend that started to form at point B was not confirmed by top C; nor was there any confirmation of the downtrend that started to form from D to E. This price formation is a struggle between buyers and sellers that has not been decided yet, and the same can be said for the price formation directly above it.

CHAPTER 5

Inverted Head-and-Shoulders Identification Exercise

Figure 5E.1. Yes. The left shoulder is formed by the two bottoms at point A, the head appears at point C, and the right shoulder appears at point E. (You may want to turn the chart upside down to help you visualize this formation.)

Figure 5E.2. Yes. The left shoulder is formed by the bottom at point A, the head appears at bottom point C, and the right shoulder appears at bottom point E.

Figure 5E.3. No. To qualify as an inverted head-and-shoulders formation, the ascent from the head (point C) to the top at point D did not go far enough. It should have gone higher than the level of the bottom at point A. This is an uptrend, which was established at bottom E and confirmed at bottom G.

Figure 5E.4. Yes. This formation has two left shoulders at points A and C, a head at point E, and a right shoulder at point G.

Rounding-Bottom Identification Exercise

Figure 5E.5. Yes. This is an example of a very slight downtrend being converted gradually into an uptrend.

Figure 5E.6. Yes. This is an example of the gradual conversion of a downtrend into an uptrend after a period of time when supply and demand were in balance.

Figure 5E.7. No. This figure represents a downtrend changing directly into an uptrend with no interval of time when the supply and demand were in relative balance. To illustrate this direct change, draw a line through the descending tops in the left half of the figure. Then draw a line through the ascending bottoms in the right half of the figure. These lines will intersect at a right angle indicating that the change in direction was immediate, and there was no interval of relative balance between the supply and demand.

Figure 5E.8. Yes. Although the price swings are greater within this formation, there are three descending tops on the left side of the figure and three ascending bottoms on the right side. In between, the price vacillates horizon-tally until the uptrend begins to develop.

Ascending-Triangle Identification Exercise

Figure 5E.9. Yes. Draw a line through the points at A, B, D, F, and H, and the top of the triangle will appear. Then draw another line through the bottom points at C, E, and G; the ascending bottom of the triangle appears. There is no need to draw the third vertical side of the triangle because it does not define the boundaries of the struggle between the buyers and the sellers. It is not neccessary for the top points of the triangle to be at the same level.

Figure 5E.10. No. This formation does not qualify as an ascending triangle because each of the top points is lower than the preceding tops.

Figure 5E.11. Yes. The top points B, D, and F are approximately level and horizontal. The line drawn through points A, C, E, and G ascends toward the horizontal top of the triangle. A large ascending triangle like this one tends to have more significant price trend implications than a small or medium-sized one; a breakout through the roof of this type of large triangle has the potential to result in a long-term upward price trend.

Figure 5E.12. Yes. Points A through H delineate the horizontal top of the triangle, and points B through I provide the ascending bottom. However, this triangle has lost its significance because the price worked its way out through the apex.

Double-Bottom Identification Exercise

Figure 5E.13. Yes. Bottoms A and C are at approximately the same price level, and intervening peak B has been surpassed by the price rise from point C.

Figure 5E.14. Yes. Bottoms A and C are at approximately the same price level, and intervening peak B has been exceeded by the price rise from point C.

Figure 5E.15. Yes. Bottoms A and C are at the same level, and intervening price peak B has been surpassed by the price rise from point C. The higher bottom at point D is the first sign that an uptrend is developing even before the rise of the price above point B.

Figure 5E.16. No. Although bottoms A and C are at the same price level, the price rise from point C never surpassed the price level at point B. In addition the price decline from point D went below the price at bottoms A and C.

Triple-Bottom Identification Exercise

Figure 5E.17. Yes. The bottoms at A, C, and E are at approximately the same price level, and the price rise from bottom E has surpassed the price peaks at points B and D.

Figure 5E.18. No. The middle bottom at point C is considerably lower than the other two bottoms at points A and E. Because of this, the figure is more accurately described as an inverted head-and-shoulders formation. (The left shoulder is bottom A, the head is bottom C, and the right shoulder is bottom E.)

Figure 5E.19. No. Bottom C is considerably higher than bottom A, and bottom E is considerably higher than bottom C. Therefore, this figure is more accurately described as an uptrend.

Figure 5E.20. Yes. Bottoms A, C, and E are at approximately the same level and the price rise from point E has surpassed the two intervening price peaks at points B and D.

CHAPTER 6
Symmetrical Triangle Identification Exercise

Figure 6E.1. Yes. Top C is lower than top A, so a downslanting top line can be drawn. Bottom D is higher than bottom B, so an upslanting bottom line can be drawn. If the price rise from point D continues and breaks out above the line drawn through points A and C, this triangle will have functioned as a continuation formation.

Figure 6E.2. No. Tops A and C are at approximately the same level, so a line drawn through them will be horizontal, not descending. Since a line drawn through bottoms B and D will slant upward, this is an ascending triangle. If the price rise from point D continues, this triangle will become a continuation formation.

Figure 6E.3. Yes. This triangle has an upward bias because a line drawn through bottoms B, D, and F slants upward more sharply than a line drawn through tops A, C, and E slants downward. It is worthwhile noting an upward bias in a triangle because it indicates that the buyers are more anxious than the sellers, and the breakout therefore has a higher probability of being through the upside.

Figure 6E.4. Yes. Here is another illustration of a symmetrical triangle with a bias, but this time it is toward the downside. The line drawn through tops B and D slants downward more sharply than the line drawn through bottoms A and C slants upward.

Figure 6E.5. Yes. A line drawn through tops B and D slants downward, and a line drawn through bottoms A, C, and E slants upward. This is a comparatively large triangle. The more time (sidewise distance) and the more price fluctuation (vertical distance) within the boundaries of a triangle, the more significant a price breakout is likely to be.

Figure 6E.6. No. While a line drawn through tops B and D is descending, a line drawn through bottoms A and C is horizontal. This triangle is therefore classed as a descending triangle. If the price decline from point D continues, this triangle will have served as a continuation formation.

Rectangle/Trading Range Identification Exercise

Figure 6E.7. Yes. Tops A, C, E, G, and I are at the approximate same price level, and a horizontal line can be drawn through them. Bottoms B, D, F, and H are at the approximate same price level, and a horizontal line can be drawn through them. These two lines are parallel to each other and define the boundaries of the trading range with resistance at the upper level and support at the lower level.

Figure 6E.8. Yes. A horizontal line can be drawn through the tops, and another horizontal line can be drawn through the bottoms, creating parallel lines.

Figure 6E.9. No. Tops C through K are each lower than the preceding tops. This sequence of declining tops meets our definition of a downtrend, however slight.

Figure 6E.10. Yes. There are three tops that can be connected by a horizontal line and three bottoms that can be connected by a horizontal line parallel to the upper line. However, this formation could also become a triple-top formation if the final price decline continues below the price at point F.

CHAPTER 8

Buy or Sell Exercise

Figure 8E.1. Buy. This is an upside breakout above the resistance level at 13½. Since the breakout occurred on a large increase in trading volume, the stock qualifies for purchase.

Figure 8E.2. Buy. This is an upside breakout from a double bottom. When the price went above the top of the intervening peak between the two bottoms on an increase in trading volume, it qualified for purchase.

Figure 8E.3. Sell. This is a breakout from a double top. The price has declined past the intervening valley floor level price of 13 ¾ and qualifies for selling.

Figure 8E.4. Buy. This is an upside breakout from a downtrend on increased volume, so it qualifies for purchase. However, a conservative investor could prefer to wait until the price establishes another bottom above $10 per share. This second bottom would then establish an uptrend.

Figure 8E.5. Sell. This is a breakout from a head and shoulders top. The price has fallen below the neckline (drawn through the bottoms at 11 and 12½). This downside breakout does not require a volume increase to qualify it for selling.

Figure 8E.6. Buy. This is an upside breakout from a symmetrical triangle on a volume increase. The stock therefore qualifies for purchase.

Figure 8E.7. Buy. This is an upside breakout from an ascending triangle on increased volume and qualifies for purchase.

Figure 8E.8. Sell. This is a downside breakout from a descending triangle. It qualifies for selling.

Figure 8E.9. Buy. This is an upside breakout from a rounding bottom. An uptrend and an increase in volume have developed, so the stock qualifies for purchase.

Figure 8E.10. Sell. This is a downside breakout from a rounding top. A downtrend has been established, so the stock qualifies for selling.

Figure 8E.11. Buy. This is an upside breakout from a head-and-shoulders bottom. The breakout occurred on a large increase in volume and an uptrend has been established. This stock is qualified for purchase.

Figure 8E.12. Sell. This is a downside breakout from a rectangle or it could also be called a triple top. In either case, the support level between 9 ¾ and 10 has been broken, so the stock qualifies for selling.

Figure 8E.13. Buy. This is an upside breakout from a triple bottom, or it could also be called a rectangle. In either case, the price has risen above the resistance level at the approximate price of 13 on increased volume; it therefore qualifies for purchase.

Figure 8E.14. Sell. This is a downside breakout from an uptrend. This breakout and the downtrend that has already established itself qualify the stock for selling.

Figure 8E.15. Buy. This is an upside breakout from a trading range or it could be called a rectangle with a resistance level of 13 ¼. Breaking through this resistance level on increased volume qualifies the stock for purchase.

Figure 8E.16. Sell. This is a downside breakout from a triple top. A downtrend was also established during the decline from the third top. The stock qualifies for selling.

Sell or Hold Exercise

Figure 8E.17. Sell A. Hold B. Stock A qualifies for selling since the price has broken out to the downside of a rectangle or trading range. Stock B qualifies for holding since the price has broken out above the resistance level at 12 ½ on increased volume.

Figure 8E.18. Sell A. Hold B. Stock A qualifies for selling since the price has broken out to the downside of a double top. Stock B qualifies for holding because the price is within an ascending triangle. Patience could be rewarded in this type of situation because ascending triangles usually breakout to the upside.

Figure 8E.19. Hold A. Sell B. Stock A qualifies for holding because it is in an uptrend that has not been broken. Stock B has broken out from an uptrend so it qualifies for selling.

Figure 8E.20. Sell A. Hold B. Stock A has made a rounding top and has established a downtrend, so it qualifies for selling. Stock B qualifies for holding because the price is within a symmetrical triangle; since this triangle was approached from below, the breakout is more likely to be on the upside (because symmetrical triangles usually serve as continuation formations).

Figure 8E.21. Sell A. Hold B. Stock A qualifies for selling because it is in a downtrend. Stock B is within a rectangle that was approached from below. Since most rectangles serve as continuation formations, the stock qualifies for holding for a while. However, if the price remains between the established support and resistance levels, this rectangle could become an elongated trading range. Because such trading ranges can last a long time, there should be a limit to your patience with this type of situation.

Figure 8E.22. Hold A. Sell B. Stock A has completed a symmetrical triangle and the price has exited through the apex of the triangle. This stock qualifies for holding to see whether the next trend will be up or down. Stock B qualifies for selling because the price has broken out of an uptrend.

Figure 8E.23. Sell A. Hold B. Stock A qualifies for selling since this is a descending triangle from which a breakout to the downside has already occurred. Stock B qualifies for holding. This stock price is within a rectangle that was approached from below. Since most rectangles serve as continuation formations, the price should breakout to the upside. However, if this rectangle extends itself into an elongated trading range, there should be a limit to your patience.

Figure 8E.24. Hold A. Sell B. Stock A formed a descending triangle and is exiting through the apex; this stock qualifies for holding to see whether the next trend will be up or down. Stock B has broken out from a double top; it therefore qualifies for selling.

Figure 8E.25. Sell A. Hold B. Stock A has broken out to the downside of a head-and-shoulders top; it therefore qualifies for selling. Stock B is in an uptrend, and therefore qualifies for holding.

Figure 8E.26. Sell A. Hold B. Stock A has made a downside breakout from a symmetrical triangle and qualifies for selling. The stock on the right has made an upside breakout from a symmetrical triangle and qualifies for holding.

Buy Selection Exercise

Figure 8E.27. Buy B. Stock B is in a high-volume uptrend and qualifies for purchase. Stock A is in a downtrend and does not qualify for purchase.

Figure 8E.28. Buy A. Stock A is breaking out to the upside from a double bottom on increased volume and qualifies for purchase. Stock B is breaking out to the downside of a double top and does not qualify for purchase.

Figure 8E.29. Buy B. Stock B is making a breakout to the upside from a head-and-shoulders bottom on increased volume and qualifies for purchase.

Stock A has established an uptrend but is still below the resistance level at 13; it would only qualify for purchase if the price continues in an uptrend and goes above the resistance level.

Figure 8E.30. Buy A. Stock A has broken out from a downtrend on high volume and therefore qualifies for purchase. Stock B has also broken out from a downtrend. The volume did not increase significantly, however, so it does not qualify for purchase.

Figure 8E.31. Buy B. Stock B is making a breakout to the upside from a head-and-shoulders bottom; the volume is beginning to increase, and the stock qualifies for purchase. Stock A is making a breakout to the downside of a head-and-shoulders top. The price has established a downtrend, so this stock does not qualify for purchase.

Figure 8E.32. Buy A. Stock A has made a rounding bottom and has established an uptrend on increased volume, so it qualifies for purchase. Stock B has completed a rounding top and has established a downtrend, so it does not qualify for purchase.

Figure 8E.33. Buy A. Stock A has made an upside breakout from a rectangle on increased volume, so it qualifies for purchase. Stock B has not broken out of the rectangle, so it does not qualify for purchase.

Figure 8E.34. Buy B. Stock B has broken out to the upside from an ascending triangle on increased volume, so it qualifies for purchase. Stock A is still inside an ascending triangle, so it does not qualify for purchase.

Figure 8E.35. Buy A. Stock A has made an upside breakout from a symmetrical triangle on increased volume, so it qualifies for purchase. Stock B is exiting through the apex of a symmetrical triangle, so it does not qualify for purchase at this point.

Figure 8E.36. Stock B has broken out from a double bottom on increased volume; it qualifies for purchase. Stock A has broken out from a double bottom; the volume did not increase at the breakout, however, so it does not qualify for purchase.

Figure 8E.37. Buy A. Stock A has made a high-volume upside breakout from a rectangle, and therefore qualifies for purchase. Stock B has made an upside breakout from a rectangle; the increase in volume at the breakout was minimal, however, so it is less qualified for purchase at this point.

Price Pattern Identification

Figure 8E.38. Buy. This is a trading range (or rectangle). It qualifies for purchase because the price has just made an upside breakout on increased volume.

Figure 8E.39. Sell. This is a head-and-shoulders top. It qualifies for selling because the neckline at 11½ has been penetrated to the downside.

Figure 8E.40. Buy. This is an uptrend with expanding volume. The uptrend has been established by the second bottom and confirmed by the third bottom. It therefore qualifies for purchase.

Figure 8E.41. Sell. This is a symmetrical triangle. It qualifies for selling because the price has broken out to the downside before reaching the apex.

Figure 8E.42. Buy. This is a triple bottom. This stock qualifies for purchase because the price has risen above the resistance level at 11, and the volume increased during this breakout.

Figure 8E.43. Wait. This is a trading range. The volume of trading within this pattern has remained low, reflecting a lack of investor interest. The price remains within the trading range. You should not buy the stock at this point. If you owned this stock, there should be a limit to your patience, since the stock price could stay in this trading range for a long time.

Figure 8E.44. Sell. This is a rounding top. A downtrend has been established, so the stock qualifies for selling.

Figure 8E.45. Buy. This is an ascending triangle. The price has made a breakout to the upside on increased volume, so the stock qualifies for purchase.

Figure 8E.46. Sell. This is a double top. The price has broken the support level at 11 ¼, so the stock qualifies for selling.

Figure 8E.47. Wait. This is an ascending triangle. The price is exiting the triangle through the apex. This is a neutral price movement, so you should wait for more definitive price and volume data before you decide what to do.

Figure 8E.48. Sell. This is a rectangle (or trading range). The price has broken to the downside of the support level at 10, so the stock qualifies for selling.

Figure 8E.49. Buy. This is a rounding bottom. An uptrend has been established and the trading volume has increased, so the stock qualifies for purchase.

Figure 8E.50. Wait. This is a descending triangle. The price is exiting the triangle through the apex. This is a neutral price movement, so you should wait for more significant price and volume data before you decide what to do.

Figure 8E.51. Buy. This is a head-and-shoulders bottom (inverted head-and-shoulders). The price has risen above the neckline resistance level at 12 and the volume has increased, so the stock qualifies for purchase.

Figure 8E.52. Sell. This is a downtrend. The downtrend has been established by the second top and confirmed by the third top. This stock qualifies for selling.

Figure 8E.53. Wait. This is a symmetrical triangle. The price is exiting through the apex of the triangle. This is a neutral price movement, so you should wait for more meaningful price and volume data before deciding what to do.

Figure 8E.54. Buy. This is a double bottom. The price has risen above the resistance level at 11 and the volume increased. This stock is qualified for purchase.

Figure 8E.55. Sell. This is a triple top. The price has fallen below the support level at 11 ½, so the stock is qualified for selling.

Figure 8E.56. Wait. This is a symmetrical triangle. The price remains within the triangle boundaries. This is a neutral situation, so you should wait for additional price and volume data before deciding what to do.

CHAPTER 10

Accumulation Exercise

Pair #1. Stock #1 is the better buy. It has had six months of the fastest rate of accumulation, and its float is small. Whereas, stock #2 had a neutral accumulation rating (no accumulation). In addition, its float is much larger.

Pair #2. Stock #1 is the better buy. While the float is the same for both stocks, stock #1 had the stronger accumulation rating for the eight months. Therefore, its float would shrink faster, creating an earlier onset of buying pressure to drive the price upward.

Pair #3. Stock #2 is the better buy. Although its float is larger, it has had seven months of slow accumulation. On the other hand, the accumulation rating for stock #1 has been neutral, so no accumulation has been done. Slow accumulation is better than none.

Pair #4. Stock #1 is the better buy. The time period and rate of accumulation has been the same for both stocks. However, the float is smaller for stock #1, so it should reach the point where buying pressure begins to build up sooner.

Pair #5. Stock #2 is the better buy. The rate of accumulation is slow, but its float is very small. With six months of accumulation already completed, buying pressure is building up. Stock #2 has a float which is 100 times as large. Even with a fast rate of accumulation, it could take years before the accumulation has any effect on the price of the stock. In the interim, if any bad news, i.e., unexpected by the accumulators, develops for this stock, the price could go much lower with that huge supply, because demand could dry up.

Pair #6. Neither stock is a good buy. Their C ratings indicate no accumulation has occurred for a year. The best informed investors have no interest in either one, and neither should you.

Distribution Exercise

Pair #1. Stock #1 is more susceptible to a price decline. It is being distributed at a fast pace. Stock #2 is not being distributed, so it is less susceptible to a decline.

Pair #2. Stock #1 is more susceptible to a price decline. It is being distributed faster than stock #2.

Pair #3. Stock #2 is more susceptible to a price decline. Although both are being distributed at a fast pace, stock #2 has been under distribution for twice as long. Its float has therefore expanded faster than the float of stock #1. As supply increases relative to demand, vulnerability to a decline increases accordingly.

Pair #4. Neither stock is more susceptible to a price decline than the other. Since neither is under distribution, the vulnerability of either one remains unknown.

Pair #5. Stock #1 is more susceptible to a price decline, because it is being distributed at a faster rate. Its float is now larger than the float of Stock #2 and is therefore more susceptible to selling pressure.

Pair #6. Stock #1 is more susceptible to price decline. Although the rate of expansion of the float is the same for both stocks, stock #1 started from a higher base, so its current float is larger than that of stock #2.

CHAPTER 11

Interpretation Exercise: Buy, Wait, or Reject?

Figure 11E.1. Buy. The indicators are positive.

Figure 11E.2. Reject. There isn't much hope for a recovery in price. The greater likelihood is that the price will drift lower or into a trading range. For further details see the interpretation and conclusion for Example 11.2.

Figure 11E.3. Wait. If this stock breaks up through the resistance level, you would be buying it at the beginning of a potentially large capital gain. However, if it is unable to make the breakthrough in a reasonable amount of time, look elsewhere for a better opportunity.

Figure 11E.4. Reject. The main reason for skepticism is the small amount of accumulation and the large floating supply. In addition, there is no increase in volume to confirm the breakout, so it has the appearance of a false start. A breakout is not a reliable indicator when it is not confirmed by any of the other indicators.

Figure 11E.5. Reject. If you bought this one you would be bottom fishing. The final bottom could be much lower than your guess. For further details see the interpretation for Example 11.5.

Figure 11E.6. Buy. The increasing volume on the breakout above the resistance level and through the moving average makes the uptrend impressive. With all the accumulation which has occurred, there's a good chance for a major long-term capital gain. For more information, see Example 11.6.

Figure 11E.7. Reject. The low trading volume signifying little interest in this stock indicates the stock will probably remain in the trading range for a long time. The lack of accumulation and the large floating supply is another warning to keep your distance from this one. Review Example 11.7 for more details.

Figure 11E.8. Buy. Here's a case of a double breakout above a resistance level and a moving average on a large increase in volume. Other favorable signs are the extended period of accumulation and the small floating supply.

The steepness of the uptrend implies a large price advance in the intermediate term.

Figure 11E.9. Reject. The slow price decline within the trading range is a negative sign. The slow distribution and the large floating supply also have negative implications. The price could weaken further and break through the support level. Don't risk your money or waste your time on this type of uncompromising situation.

Figure 11E.10. Wait. The long period of accumulation and the small floating supply carry positive implications. The volume rising and falling with the price also are signs of price appreciation potential. Since the moving average is lining up with the resistance level, a breakout would occur through both simultaneously. Buy "at the market" when the breakout occurs.

Figure 11E.11. Wait. If this pattern becomes a rounding bottom, the capital appreciation potential is large. Since accumulation has been persistent and is increasing, the prospects for a breakout above the moving average are improving. In this type of situation, you may buy as soon as the moving average is penetrated to the upside and an uptrend is established.

Interpretation Exercise: Hold or Sell?

Figure 11E.12. Sell. The first sign of trouble is the fast rate of distribution. With the penetration of the uptrend line and the moving average and the establishment of the downtrend, there's no reason to hold this stock. The increasing volume of trading in the downtrend suggests the decline will be steep.

Figure 11E.13. Hold. When a stock price is rising steeply, the most positive way for that rise to end is by conversion into a lower, more sustainable rate of ascent. The uptrend line was broken, but the moving average is intact, indicating that the price could continue trending upward more slowly for some time.

Figure 11E.14. Hold. The accumulation rating of B suggests this stock price has potential to rise further. You should remain alert to the possibility of a rounding top. The signs to look for are a switch to a distribution rating of D or E and a volume increase accompanied by a stalling out of the price rise. If they develop, sell.

Figure 11E.15. Hold. Although the uptrend line has been broken, the symmetrical triangle which developed subsequently could be a continuation pattern. With an accumulation rating of B there's reason to hope a new uptrend will develop. If the price were to break down through the triangle boundary line and the moving average, it should then be sold.

Figure 11E.16. Hold. The accumulation rating of A provides one positive sign suggesting an upside breakout from the rectangle. Unlike a triangle, which usually results in a new price trend up or down, the rectangle could be the initial phase of an extended trading range. If this should be the next development, or if the accumulation rating were to decline to C or lower, there should be a limit to your patience.

Figure 11E.17. Hold. The ascending triangle, combined with the accumulation within it, are positive indicators that the stock will resume an upward trend. If the price, however, should penetrate the bottom boundary of the triangle and the moving average, it should be sold.

Figure 11E.18. Hold. The penetration of the trend line is a negative sign. The fluctuation of the accumulation/distribution indicator reflects the uncertainties of the situation. Long-term uptrends are frequently interrupted by shorter downward moves. In these situations, the long moving average becomes the key indicator. If it is penetrated, the stock should be sold.

Figure 11E.19. Hold. The most negative aspect of this situation is the switch from slow accumulation to slow distribution. If this movement persists or increases, the implication is that a top is forming. The absence of an increase in the trading volume gives some hope that a top is not forming. The downside penetration of the uptrend has not been confirmed by the penetration of the moving average. With this balance between the positive and negative signs, holding is justified. If the moving average, though, is penetrated, the stock should be sold.

Figure 11E.20. Hold. The high rate of distribution and the descending triangle are negative signs. The situation should be watched closely. Simultaneous penetration of the bottom of the triangle and the moving average is likely. Hold on to see what happens, but protect your profit with a stop loss order under the moving average.

Figure 11E.21. Hold. A stock price in a parabolic curve is a beautiful thing to experience if you own it. But the beauty of the smooth rise conceals the potential hazard of a free falling price. What goes straight up often comes straight back down. Protection of your profit should be given top priority. This can be done while still holding the stock by placing a progressive stop loss order each morning after the price has entered its vertical ascent phase. See Figure 11.21 for demonstration of the advantage of a short moving average in this situation.

Figure 11E.22. Hold. The stock price is flat for the time being. The next bit of news about the company will determine the future trend. Protect your profit with a stop loss order under the moving average.

Appendix B

GLOSSARY

ACCUMULATION—Purchases of large quantities of shares in anticipation of a major rise in the price of the stock. This is done by those with superior knowledge of the company who believe the stock is greatly underpriced.

ADVISORY LETTER—A letter containing advice for investors. These letters are published by individuals or companies and are distributed to their subscribers. The letters contain advice for buying, selling, or holding specific investments.

AMERICAN STOCK EXCHANGE—This exchange primarily lists small and medium sized companies. Its requirements for listing a company are less than those for listing on the N.Y. Stock Exchange and the volume of trading is much lower. Address: 86 Trinity Place, N.Y., NY 10006.

ASCENDING TRIANGLE—A stock price pattern characterized by two or more tops at the same approximate level and two or more bottoms, with each successive bottom being higher than the preceding bottom. A line drawn across the tops will be met by the ascending line drawn across the bottoms. These two lines form an upward slanted wedge (see Figures 5.7 and 5.8 for examples).

AT THE MARKET—A term used in entering a buy or sell order. It tells the broker to buy immediately at the best available price from any seller or to sell immediately for the best available price to any buyer.

BEAR—An investor who believes the price of a stock is going to decline.

BEAR MARKET—A period of time (usually from six months to several years) during which stock averages trend lower and lower, and any upward price movement is relatively short in duration.

BEAR TRAP—A short-lived breakthrough of a support level followed by an extended rise in price. An investor observing the price decline through the support would expect it to fall further and could be misled into selling the stock too soon.

BETA RATING—A number which rates the volatility of a stock's price relative to Standard and Poor's index of 500 stocks. A value of 1.0 indicates the stock's price fluctuation is equal to that of the index. A value of 1.5 indicates the stock's price would go up or down one-and-a-half times as much (150 percent). A value of .5 indicates the stock's price would go up or down one-half as much (50 percent).

BLACK INK—This term refers to the financial condition of producing a profit. This condition results when the total amount of income generated by a company exceeds all of its expenses.

BOTTOM—A succession of prices which fall to a low point and then rise from the low point for at least several days. The lowest point in this sequence of prices is called the bottom.

BOTTOMING OUT—This phrase describes the process by which an extended downtrend is converted into an uptrend. This change in direction can occur in one day, it can take a few days, or it can take several years to complete. Usually, however, the bottoming out process involves the formation of a double bottom, a triple bottom, an inverted head-and-shoulders, a triangle, a rectangle, or a rounding bottom.

BREAKOUT/BREAKTHROUGH—The penetration of a trendline, neckline, or formation boundary line by 5 percent or more by the close of business for the day.

BULL—An investor who believes the price of a stock is going to rise.

BULL MARKET—A period of time (usually from one year to several years) during which stock averages trend higher and higher, and any downward price movement is relatively short in duration.

BULL TRAP—A short-lived breakout above a resistance level followed by an extended decline in price. An investor observing the rise through the resistance would expect the price to continue rising and could be misled into buying the stock too soon.

BUY SIGNAL—The signal given when a stock price breakout occurs to the upside of a trendline, neckline, or formation boundary line. This buy signal has the most significance when it is confirmed by a large increase in the trading volume. (See Figures 4.3, 5.1, 5.3, 5.4, 5.7, 5.9–5.11 for examples.)

CAPITAL GAIN—The amount of profit made on a transaction. When the stock goes up in price after purchase, the sale price will be greater than the purchase price, and this difference is the capital gain.

CHURN AN ACCOUNT—Excessive trading which results in losses for the investor and large commissions for the broker. SEC regulations prohibit a broker from churning a customer's account.

CLOSELY HELD STOCK—Shares held by organizations or major stockholders who want to maintain ownership in the company and do not intend to trade them in the foreseeable future.

COMMON STOCK—The basic form of ownership in a corporation which entitles the owner to voting rights and a proportionate share of dividends.

CONSOLIDATION—A period of relative balance between supply and demand during which price fluctuations are limited. When the relationship becomes unbalanced, the price moves either up or down. Triangles and rectangles are common forms of consolidation patterns.

CONTINUATION FORMATION—A pattern that forms when the supply of a stock and the demand for it are relatively equal. When the price of the stock approaches from one direction and exits in the same direction, that pattern is called a continuation formation. (See Figures 6.1–6.4, 6.7, and 6.8 for examples.)

CYCLICAL INDUSTRY—An industry whose profits rise and fall with the economic cycle. When the economy is doing well, the companies in a cyclical industry prosper. When the economy does poorly, profits decline or may disappear.

DEMAND—The total volume of a company's shares sought for purchase by buyers. The amount of this volume is usually in a constant state of change. When the amount of shares sought for purchase is substantially greater than the number of shares available for sale, the price per share tends to rise.

DESCENDING TRIANGLE—A stock price pattern characterized by two or more bottoms at the approximate same level and two or more tops with each successive top being lower than the preceding top. A line drawn across the bottoms will be met by the descending line drawn across the tops. These two lines form a downward slanting wedge. (See Figure 3.20 for an example.) The third side of the triangle is not drawn because it does not serve to define the boundaries of the price fluctuation.

DISTRIBUTION—Sales of large quantities of shares of a stock in anticipation of a major decline in the price. These sales are made by those with superior knowledge about the company who believe the stock is greatly overpriced.

DOUBLE BOTTOM—The pattern formed when the price of a stock which has made one bottom, declines again to the same approximate level, and then rises once again. (See Figures 5.9 and 5.10 for examples.)

DOUBLE TOP—The pattern formed when the price of a stock which has peaked once, rises again to the same approximate level, and then retreats once more. (See Figures 3.10–3.14 for examples.)

DOWNTICK—A stock trade at a price lower than the preceding price. If the current price is 10 dollars a share, a subsequent trade at $9\frac{7}{8}$ or lower is a downtick.

DOWNTREND LINE—A line drawn through two or more descending tops. (See Figures 4.1–4.3 for examples.)

FLOATING SUPPLY—The amount of outstanding shares which are not closely held by organizations or individuals who want to maintain their ownership in the company.

FUNDAMENTALIST—An investor who makes buy and sell decisions based on the financial reports on a company and the competitive and economic factors that affect its prospects for making profits.

HEAD-AND-SHOULDERS—This pattern forms when the price of a stock rises to a peak, declines, then rises to a second peak higher than the first, declines again, then rises to a third peak which is lower than the second peak. This sequence of prices gives the rough appearance of a left shoulder, a head in the middle, and a right shoulder. (See Figures 3.5–3.7 for examples.)

HOT TIP—This is a story about a company. The person telling you this story usually implies that the story is not yet available to the general public via the mass media. Stories passed along in this manner are often inaccurate or erroneous and are therefore a poor basis for making investment decisions.

INSIDE TRADING—An inside trade is one made prior to the public release of material information capable of moving the price up or down significantly. SEC regulations prohibit inside trading and prescribe fines and jail time for violations of these regulations.

INTERMEDIATE TERM—When discussing stock price movements, this term can refer to a period of time as short as two months or as long as six months.

ISSUED SHARES—The total number of shares created by the company.

LONG TERM—When discussing stock price movements, this term refers to a period of six months or longer.

MOVING AVERAGE—An average price calculated for a specific number of days. Each business day a new average is calculated and plotted on a price and volume chart for the stock. For detailed information on how to construct and plot the average see Chapter 9.

NASDAQ—See National Association of Securities Dealers Automated Quotation system.

NATIONAL ASSOCIATION OF SECURITIES DEALERS AUTOMATED QUOTATION SYSTEM—A national electronic network of automated stock quotation display devices. It provides current price quotes for many stocks which are not listed on the stock exchanges.

NECKLINE—The line that can be drawn through the two bottom points of the two valleys between the head and shoulders of a head-and-shoulders formation. (See Figures 3.5–3.9 for examples.)

NEW YORK STOCK EXCHANGE—The largest exchange in the United States.

It lists most of the largest, best known companies, and also many medium and smaller ones. It has the highest listing standards. Address: 11 Wall Street, N.Y., NY 10005.

ONE-DAY REVERSAL—A sudden change of direction in the price movement of a stock at the end of an intermediate or long-term trend. In accord with its name, this change of direction occurs within one trading day.

OUTSTANDING SHARES—The total number of shares released from the company treasury.

OVERBOUGHT—A condition which occurs when buyers have been very aggressive in purchasing a stock. These overly hopeful buyers drive the price of the stock up too high too fast, and this high price becomes very susceptible to a period of decline.

OVERSOLD—A condition which occurs when sellers have been willing to take whatever they can get for selling their stock. These overly fearful sellers cause the price of the stock to fall too low too fast, and the price eventually becomes ready to rise to higher levels.

PARABOLIC CURVE—This phenomenon occurs when a stock price rise accelerates until it is going up in almost a straight line. Such an event can only last a short time, and the usual consequence is an extended decline from the peak price.

PENETRATION—The action of a stock price when it breaks through from one side of a boundary or trendline to the other side.

PROFIT MARGIN—The excess of income over expenses. A company's profit margin will fluctuate over the years. When there are few companies in a young industry, the profit margin will usually be high. As more competitors enter the industry (because of the high profits), profit margins tend to shrink.

RECTANGLE/TRADING RANGE—This price pattern occurs when buyers are convinced that a stock price is a bargain at a certain level, and sellers are convinced the stock is overpriced at a higher level. As long as these buyer and seller attitudes prevail, the price will rise from the lower level and fall from the higher level. After these fluctuations have occurred two times, two horizontal and parallel lines can be drawn through the top prices and the bottom prices. These lines then delineate the temporary trading range for the price of the stock. (See Figures 6.7–6.9 for examples.)

RED INK—This term is used to describe the financial result when the company's expenses are larger than its income and it is losing money.

RESISTANCE LEVEL—The highest price in a trading range (see Figures 6.7–6.9 for examples). This term can also refer to the highest price in any chart formation whose top boundary is a horizontal line.

REVERSAL FORMATION—Any of several patterns that form while the direction of price movement is changing from upward to downward or from downward to upward. The price of the stock approaches the pattern from one direction but exits the pattern in the opposite direction. (See Figures 5.7, 6.5, and 6.9 for examples.)

ROOF LINE—This term refers to the horizontal line that represents the top side of any price pattern or formation. (See Figures 5.7 and 5.8 for examples.)

ROUNDING BOTTOM—The saucer-shaped curve that develops when a downtrend in a stock price gradually changes into an uptrend over a period of several months or longer. (See Figures 5.5 and 5.6 for examples.)

ROUNDING TOP—The upside-down saucer-shaped curve which develops when an uptrend in a stock price gradually changes into a downtrend over a period of several months or longer. (See Figures 3.18 and 3.19 for examples.)

RUMOR—This is a favorable or unfavorable statement about a company that has not been verified by an authorized official of that company.

SELL SIGNAL—The signal given when a stock price breaks through to the downside of a trendline, neckline, or a formation boundary line. This signal has the most significance when it occurs in conjunction with a large increase in the trading volume. (See Figures 3.5–3.10, 3.17, and 3.20.)

SHORT TERM—Any period of time up to approximately two months long.

SPIKE—A quick up and down price movement which has the appearance of an upright spike on a price chart.

STOCK CHART—This chart displays the price and volume fluctuations of a company's stock over a period of time.

STOP ORDER—An order to buy or sell a stock when the price reaches a specified price. When that happens, the stop order is executed as an order to buy or sell at the market.

SUPPLY—The total volume of a company's shares available for sale. The amount of this volume varies continually. When the supply is substantially greater than the demand, there is downward pressure on the price of the stock.

SUPPORT LEVEL—The lowest price in a trading range (see Figures 6.7–6.9). This term can also refer to the lowest price in any formation whose lower boundary line is horizontal.

SYMMETRICAL TRIANGLE—This type of triangle is formed when price fluctuations result in two or more consecutive descending tops and two or more consecutive ascending bottoms. A straight declining line drawn across the tops will be met by a straight ascending line drawn across the bottoms. These two lines form a wedge-shaped figure (see Figures 6.1–6.6). The third side of the triangle is not drawn, because it does not serve to define the boundaries of the price fluctuation.

TECHNICAL ANALYSIS—The use of price and volume charts as the basis for investment decisions. The rationale for this approach is that the price and volume information in the chart reflects all that is known about the company by all the interested parties who have bought or sold that stock. Since the stock chart summarizes and displays the net result of all these buy and sell decisions, it is the best single resource for making rational investment decisions.

TOP—A top is formed when a succession of stock prices rise, reach a high point, and then decline for several days. The highest point in this sequence is called the top.

TOPPING OUT—This phrase describes the process by which an extended uptrend is converted into a downtrend. This change in direction can occur in one day, it can take a few days, or it can take several years to complete. The topping out process usually involves the formation of a double top, a triple top, a head-and-shoulders, a triangle, a rectangle, or a rounding top.

TRADING VOLUME—The daily trading volume is the number of shares traded in the course of the business day. These figures are published in most daily newspapers.

TREND LINE—A line drawn through two or more ascending bottoms or through two or more descending tops. The former line will trend upward, and the price is said to be in an uptrend. (See Figures 2.1–2.4 for examples.) The latter line trends downward and the price is said to be in a downtrend. (See Figures 4.1–4.3 for examples.)

TRIPLE BOTTOM—This pattern is formed when the price of a stock which has made a double bottom declines again to the same approximate level and then rises again (see Figures 5.10 and 5.11).

TRIPLE TOP—This pattern is formed when the price of a stock which has made a double top rises again to the same approximate level and then falls again (see Figures 3.15–3.17).

UPTICK—A trade at a price higher than the previous price. If the current price is 10 dollars a share, a subsequent trade at 10⅛ or higher is an uptick.

UPTREND LINE—A line drawn through two or more ascending bottoms (see Figures 2.1–2.4).

VALLEY FLOOR—This is a horizontal line drawn through the bottom point between two consecutive tops (see Figures 3.10–3.14).

V-SHAPED BOTTOM—This price pattern occurs when a sharp downtrend suddenly changes into a sharp uptrend (see Figure 5.2).

VOLATILE—The tendency to fluctuate more widely in price than the average stock. See BETA RATING for details on how the volatility of a stock is given a numerical rating.

W-SHAPED BOTTOM—Another name for a double bottom (see Figures 5.8 and 5.9).

Appendix C
BIBLIOGRAPHY

Burgauer, James. *The Do-It-Yourself Investor*. Chicago: Probus Publishing, 1987.

Downes, John and Goodman, Jordan. *Barron's Finance and Investment Handbook*. Woodbury, NY: Barron's Education Services, 1986.

Engel, Louis and Brendan, Boyd. *How to Buy Stocks*. Boston: Little, Brown and Co., 1982.

Fosback, Norman G. *Stock Market Logic*. Fort Lauderdale, FL: Institute for Econometric Research, 1976.

Jilor, William. *How Charts Can Help You in the Stock Market*. New York: Commodity Research Publishing, 1961.

Packer, Rod E. *Stock Trading Software Guide*. Reston, VA: Reston Publishing Co., 1985.

Pistolese, Clifford. *Nerves of Steel*. Chicago: Probus Publishing, 1993.

Pring, Martin J. *Technical Analysis Explained*. New York: McGraw-Hill, 1980.

Staff of United Business Services. *Successful Investing*. New York: Simon and Schuster, 1983.

Weinstein, Stan. *Secrets for Profiting in Bull and Bear Markets*. Homewood, IL: Dow Jones-Irwin, 1987.

Weiss, Jeffrey. *Beat the Market*. New York: Cloverdale Press, 1985.

INDEX

ABOUT THE AUTHOR

Clifford Pistolese is a very successful private investor with more than thirty years of experience in stock chart construction and successful trading during all phases of market cycles. During that time he developed a charting system that has enabled him to outperform the market consistently. He is the author of the first edition of *Using Technical Analysis.*

Mr. Pistolese earned a Bachelor of Arts degree in psychology from Rutgers University where he was president of Psi Chi, the National Honor Society in Psychology. He has taken an early retirement in Florida, where he continues trading for his own account.